About the Author

Frank Cottrell Boyce started out as a screenwriter, writing episodes of the TV soap *Coronation Street*! He has also written screenplays for well-known movies, including *Millions*.

Millions is his first novel and has been published in twenty-seven languages. It was based on Frank's original screenplay for a film made by Danny Boyle. He has also written the books *Framed*, about an incredible art robbery and *Cosmic*, about a boy who goes into space by accident.

Frank used to work as an assistant at a puppet show, where he was only ever paid in small coins. He thinks this could be how he first became interested in the problems created by money that is difficult to spend.

Frank has seven children and lives with his family in Liverpool.

Millions

Frank Cottrell Boyce

Literacy evolve

Heinemann is an imprint of Pearson Education Limited, a company incorporated in England and Wales, having its registered office at Edinburgh Gate, Harlow, Essex, CM20 2JE. Registered company number: 872828

www.pearsonschools.co.uk

Heinemann is a registered trademark of Pearson Education Limited

Published by arrangement with Macmillan Children's Books Limited.
The right of Frank Cottrell Boyce to be identified as author of this Work has been asserted by him in accordance with the Copyright, Designs and Patents Act 1988.

This edition first published 2009

12 11 10 09
10 9 8 7 6 5 4 3 2 1

British Library Cataloguing in Publication Data
A catalogue record for this book is available from the British Library.

Millions
ISBN 978-0435035853

Printed in the UK by Scotprint

This is a special edition of the book for Literacy Evolve. To order further copies, please contact:
Telephone: 0845 630 22 22
Fax: 0845 630 77 77
Email: myorders@pearson.com
Web: www.pearsonschools.co.uk/literacyevolve

1

If our Anthony was telling this story, he'd start with the money. It always comes down to money, he says, so you might as well start there. He'd probably put, 'Once upon a time there were 229,370 little pounds sterling,' and go on till he got to, 'and they all lived happily ever after in a high-interest bank account.' But he's not telling this story. I am. Personally, I like to start with the patron saint of whatever it is. For instance, when we had to write about moving house for Literacy Hour, I put:

Moving House
by
Damian Cunningham, Year Five

We have just moved house to 7 Cromarty Close. The patron saint of moving house is St Anne (1st century). She was the Mother of Our Lady. Our Lady did not die but floated up into Heaven while still fairly young. St Anne was upset. To cheer her up, four angels picked up her house and took it to the seaside in Italy, where it can be seen to this day. You can pray to St Anne for help with moving house. She will watch over you, but not do actual removals. Anne is also the patron saint of miners, horse-riding, cabinetmakers and the city of Norwich. While alive, she performed many wonders.

The patron saint of this story is St Francis of Assisi (1181–1226), because it all sort of started with a robbery and the first saintish thing he ever did was a robbery. He stole some cloth from his father and gave it to the poor. There is a patron saint of actual robbers – Dismas (1st century) – but I'm not an actual robber. I was only trying to be good.

*

It was our first day at Great Ditton Primary. The sign outside says, 'Great Ditton Primary – Creating Excellence for a New Community'.

'See that?' said Dad as he left us at the gates. 'Good isn't good enough here. Excellence, that's what they're after. My instruction for the day is, "Be excellent." The instructions for supper I'll leave on the fridge door.'

One thing about me is that I always really try to do whatever Dad tells me. It's not that I think he'll go off and leave us if we're a problem, but why take that risk? So I was excellent first lesson. Mr Quinn was doing 'People We Admire' for Art. A huge boy with a freckly neck nominated Sir Alex Ferguson and listed all the trophies United had won under his stewardship. A boy called Jake said players were more important than managers and nominated Wayne Rooney for individual flair. Mr Quinn was looking around the room. To be educational about it, football was not taking him where he wanted to go. I put my hand up. He asked a girl.

'Don't know any footballers, sir.'

'It doesn't have to be a footballer.'

'Oh. Don't know, then, sir.'

I used my other hand to hoist my hand up higher.

'Damian, who do you admire?'

By now, most of the others were into players versus managers.

I said, 'St Roch, sir.'

The others stopped talking.

'Who does he play for?'

'No one, sir. He's a saint.'

The others went back to football.

'He caught the plague and hid in the woods so he wouldn't infect anyone, and a dog came and fed him every day. Then he started to do miraculous cures and people came to see him – hundreds of people – in his hut in the woods. He was so worried about saying the wrong thing to someone that he didn't say a word for the last ten years of his life.'

'We could do with a few like him in this class. Thank you, Damian.'

'He's the patron saint of plague, cholera and skin complaints. While alive, he performed many wonders.'

'Well, you learn something new.'

He was looking for someone else now, but I was enjoying being excellent. Catherine of Alexandria (4th century) came to mind. 'They wanted her to marry a king, but she said she was married to Christ. So they tried to crush her on a big wooden wheel, but it shattered into a thousand splinters – huge sharp splinters – which flew into the crowd, killing and blinding many bystanders.'

'That's a bit harsh. Collateral damage, eh? Well, thank you, Damian.'

By now everyone had stopped debating players versus managers. They were all listening to me.

'After that they chopped her head off. Which did kill her, but instead of blood, milk came spurting out of her neck. That was one of her wonders.'

'Thank you, Damian.'

'She's the patron saint of nurses, fireworks, wheel-makers and the town of Dunstable (Bedfordshire). The Catherine wheel is named after her. She's a virgin martyr. There are other great virgin martyrs. For instance, St Sexburga of Ely (670–700).'

Everyone started laughing. Everyone always laughs at that name. They probably laughed at it in 670–700 too.

'Sexburga was Queen of Kent. She had four sisters, who all became saints. They were called—'

Before I could say Ethelburga and Withburga, Mr Quinn said, 'Damian, I did say thank you.'

He actually said thank you three times. If that doesn't make me excellent, I don't know what does.

I was also an artistic inspiration, as nearly all the

boys painted pictures of the collateral damage at the execution of St Catherine. There were a lot of fatal flying splinters and milk spurting out of necks. Jake painted Wayne Rooney, but he was the only one.

In the dining hall, a boy on Hot Dinners came and waggled his burger under my nose and said, 'Sexyburger, sexyburger.' All the people round the table laughed.

I found this very unenlightening and was about to say so when Anthony came and sat by me and they all stopped.

We had ham and tomato sandwiches and two small tubes of Pringles. I said, 'I've been excellent. What about you?'

He whispered, 'You are making yourself conspicuous. You need to blend in more. People are laughing at you.'

'I don't mind being laughed at. Persecution is good for you. They laughed at Joseph of Copertino until he learned to levitate.'

The huge boy with the freckly neck came and sat down. His belly caught the end of the table and tipped it up. My tube of Pringles rolled towards him. He picked it up and opened it.

'They're his,' said Anthony, pointing at me.

'And who are you?' asked Freckle Neck.

'I'm his big brother.'

'You're not that big. All Pringles belong to me.' A dandruff of crumbs fell from his mouth. 'School policy.'

'You can't take his Pringles. He's got no mum.'

'How can he have no mum? Everyone's got a mum. Even people who've got no dad have got a mum. I'm enjoying these, by the way.'

'She's dead,' said Anthony.

Freckle Neck stopped crunching and handed my Pringles back. He said his name was Barry.

'Nice to meet you, Barry.' Anthony offered him his hand to shake. Anthony believed in making friends. 'Where do you live?' he asked.

'Over the bridge, next to the twenty-four hour.'

'Now that,' said Anthony, 'is a very sought-after area. Very sought-after.'

My brother is very, very interested in real estate.

On the way to the playground, Anthony said, 'Works every time. Tell them your mum's dead and they give you stuff.'

*

In the afternoon, for some reason, I decided to do a St Roch. I forbore all temptation to speak during Numeracy Hour – didn't put my hand up, didn't answer a tables question even when pointed at. When Mr Quinn asked me if I was OK, I was tempted to reply, but I just nodded my head instead. I wasn't contributing to the class, but I was being excellent in a different, less obvious way.

I kept this up all the way home. Dad had left instructions fixed to the fridge door with a *Clangers* magnet:

Dear Boys

Chicken and asparagus pie. The pie is in the top drawer of the freezer. Put the oven on to 190°. Go and watch Countdown. When Countdown is over, the oven will be warm enough. Put the pie in. Take your uniforms off and put them over the end of your bed. Put your tracksuits on. Then put some oven chips in. I will be home before they're cooked.

D

I enjoyed being called dear.

When Dad came home, we had the pie, followed by five pieces of fruit and a pint of water each to hydrate our livers. When they were completely hydrated, we did our homework and he sat with us. I still didn't say a word, but then the phone rang and I accidentally answered it. I don't know how St Roch kept it up for ten years, although admittedly he had it easier living in a time before phones. Anyway, it was Mr Quinn. My teacher actually rang our actual house. How excellent is that!

Later Dad came and sat on the end of the bed and said, 'You're a bit quiet today. Cat got your tongue?'

I shook my head.

'I heard you were quiet in school too.'

I nodded.

'Anything you want to tell me?'

Shook again.

'Right. Well, time for bed.'

He'd nearly closed the door when the temptation to speak finally overwhelmed me. I said, 'What did Mr Quinn want?'

'Well you know, a chat really. It was him who was telling me about how quiet you were.'

'He said thank you to me three times, so I must have been fairly excellent. Did he say I was excellent?'

'He said . . . Yes, he said you were excellent.' He ruffled my hair. 'One of the customers was telling me about this place today. It's called the Snowdrome. You can toboggan or have a go at skiing. Fancy it?'

I wasn't sure.

'For being excellent. As a reward.'

'OK, then.'

'OK. So we'll go straight from school tomorrow, because you're excellent.'

The Snowdrome was quality completely. It's real snow inside, made of ice crystals from a big blower. They give you a special snowsuit to wear when you're in there. You're not supposed to have two people on a toboggan, but Anthony explained to the man that our mum was dead and he let us do what we liked. We went down twice two together, once on our bellies and three times backwards.

In school next morning, everyone was interested to hear all about it. I explained how the ice blower worked and was giving a demonstration of backward-tobogganing when I smashed into Mr Quinn, who was coming in through the door.

'Watch it! Watch it!' he yelled as he dropped all our workbooks.

I helped him pick them up. I saw my own, the one about St Anne. It had a note stuck inside, which he took out and pocketed as he gave me back the book.

'What d'you think you're playing at, lad?'

'The Snowdrome, sir. We went. It was good.'

He suddenly looked all cheery. He said, 'Well, you could write about that for today's Literacy Hour, couldn't you? Give an exciting description of all the fun you had. No patron saint of Snowdromes, I bet.'

Speke Snowdrome
by
Damian Cunningham, Mr Quinn's Class

Speke Snowdrome is quality. You can skate or toboggan. The patron saint of skating is Lidwina (virgin martyr, 1380-1433), who was injured in a skating accident and spent the rest of her life in bed. She bore her mortification with forbearance and performed several wonders: for instance, eating nothing but Holy Communion wafers for seven years. You can read more about her at www.totallysaints.com/lidwina.html

The truth is, there is always a patron saint. As St Clare of Assisi (1194–1253) once said to me, 'Saints are like television. They're everywhere. But you need an aerial.'

2

Anthony can't believe I've got this far without mentioning European Monetary Union.

European Monetary Union
by
Anthony Cunningham, Year Six

Money was invented in China in 1100 BC. Before that Chinese merchants used knives and spades to trade with. These were too heavy to carry, so they used model knives and spades instead. These were made of bronze and were the first coins. Soon every country had its own coins. In Europe alone there were the sturdy German Deutschmark, the extravagant Italian lire, the stylish French franc and of course the Great British pound. The pound was first invented in 1489, when it was called a sovereign. On 17 December it will be replaced by the euro.

When you put an old pound in the bank, they put it on a special train that takes it to a secret location to be scrapped. Then the train comes back in the morning with new money. So right now nearly all the money in England is on trains.

You should collect your old coins in separate jam jars - one for five pees, one for tens, one for twenties and so on. When they're full, take them to the bank to exchange. 17 December is '€ Day', the day we say GOODBYE to the old pound.

Anthony said goodbye to the old pound nearly every day. On the way home from school, he used to run like mad to the middle of the footbridge, then wait there till a train went roaring by beneath us. Then he'd wave and yell until it was out of sight, just like the Railway Children, shouting, 'Goodbye! Goodbye, old pounds!'

He made it sound like every single ten-pound note was a personal friend. Sometimes you'd think he was going to cry. 'Just think,' he'd say, '500-odd years of history, up in smoke.'

Other times, he'd seem quite happy about it. 'Just think,' he'd say, 'come Christmas we'll be able to spend the same money from Galway to Greece.'

Every night before we went to bed, the three of us dropped any small coins we had into a big whisky bottle at the foot of the stairs. On the way to bed, Anthony would nearly weep as he dropped his five pees in. On the way to breakfast, he'd stroke the bottle happily and say, 'Amazing how fast it mounts up.'

Personally, I think, so what? Money's just a thing and things change. That's what I've found. One minute something's really there, right next to you, and you can cuddle up to it. The next it just melts away, like a Malteser.

3

Moving House
by
Anthony Cunningham, Year Six

We have just moved house to 7 Cromarty Close - a three-bedroomed property, not overlooked to the front. It cost £180, 000 but will retain its value well or most likely go up! It has solar panels on the roof and a cost-efficient central-heating system throughout. It has two bathrooms, inc. en suite to the master b'room. Substantial gardens front and rear complete the picture in an exclusive new development in a semi-rural setting. I've got my own bedroom at last. It's got footballer wallpaper, which I chose myself.

To be architectural about it, I found the new house disappointing.

I remember Cromarty Close when it was made of string. Dad took us to a big field near the railway, all overgrown with brambles and nettles. A man with a checked shirt and a clipboard led us to a place where the brambles had been cleared and the grass cut short. It was criss-crossed with avenues of string. He pointed down one and said, 'Dogger.' Then he walked to the corner of the next one and said, 'Finisterre.' Then he pointed off to the left and said, 'Cromarty'.

'What d'you think?' Dad said. 'Want to move here?'

I said, 'Yes, please!' very enthusiastically.

So we did.

Actually, my enthusiasm was because of a mis-understanding. I thought he was suggesting we live in the field, with the string. A lot of saints have lived in unusual houses. St Ursula (4th century) lived on a ship with 11,000 holy companions. St Simeon (390–459) tried to avoid the temptations of the world by living on top of a three-metre column. When sightseers started coming to stare at him, he moved to a ten-metre column so he wouldn't hear them. And when they just started shouting (in 449), he moved to a twenty-metre column, where he ended his days in peaceful contemplation.

Compared to that, living in a field full of brambles and string seemed sensible and pleasant. I was looking forward to it. When we came back, all the brambles had gone and there was a sign saying 'Portland Meadows – exclusive, discreet, innovative', and four rows of houses with very pointy roofs and funny-shaped windows. Number 7 Cromarty Close is a three-bedroom detached with substantial gardens and solar panels. Anthony said, 'Detached houses hold their value better and three-bedroom is the configuration most sought after by most buyers. The solar panels are added value.'

Compared to a boat with 11,000 companions, or a twenty-metre marble column, our house seemed a bit unsaintly, so I built myself a hermitage.

Dad decided to get rid of the cardboard boxes. We ripped them open and found all sorts of stuff that we'd forgotten we had. One was full of vases.

One was full of bedding. One had the Christmas decorations and a Micro Machines racing circuit inside (we set it up in the boxroom). I found the one with Mum's dresses in and her make-up.

When they were all empty, I took the boxes down to the railway, slotted them inside each other and there you go, a hermitage. It was tunnel-shaped, with little flaps for looking out. When the trains went by, the whole place shook. If it was dark, the trains lit up the inside for a second. There was a line of holly bushes between the gardens and the track, so the hermitage was nearly invisible from the houses. I took a few things down there – such as my St Francis bookmark and a tube of tinted moisturizer I found – but not much, the whole point being to live a simpler life. Not full-time, obviously, because of school. But whenever I could. I got a bit scratched going through the holly, but that was OK because suffering is good (it's called mortification).

I got the idea for the hermitage from Rose of Lima (1586–1617), who lived in one at the bottom of her parents' garden from when she was a little girl. She had multiple and marvellous visions, including those of the Blessed Virgin and the Holy Ghost, and visitations from many saints.

Personally, I didn't get any, even though I stayed there until it was really cold.

I went on Google to try and find out why my hermitage wasn't working and the answer was obvious. Not enough mortification. People like Rose of Lima didn't just live in hermitages. They fasted for weeks. They went everywhere barefoot. They wore uncomfortable clothes. They scourged themselves.

Some forms of mortification are just not practical. Fasting for seven years, for instance, is not going to happen when your dad is obsessed with everyone eating five pieces of fruit a day. And as for scourging, well, there were no facilities in Portland Meadow. But I did sleep on the floor that night. I waited until I heard Dad's light go off, then I got out of bed and lay down just under the window. It was uncomfortable, but that's the point. Then on the way to school the next morning, I let Anthony get ahead of me and slipped my shoes off. It was fine when we were walking across the field – though my socks did get wet. But the path up to the road is made of little bits of gravel. I think one of the builders must have employed someone to sharpen each bit of it before they put it on the ground. It was really, really mortifying. I was greatly tempted to walk on the grass verge, but I resisted. The pavement was easy after that.

I met Mr Quinn at the school gates. He noticed my feet and said, 'Something wrong with your shoes, Damian?'

I said, 'Mortifying my flesh, sir.'

I think he was impressed.

During Numeracy Hour Jake came and tapped me on the shoulder and then went, 'Ow!'

'Jake, what are you playing at and is it maths?' asked Mr Quinn.

'I was going to ask him for a borrow of his ruler, sir, and he's spiky.'

'What?'

Now everyone was looking at me.

Jake said, 'I just touched Damian's shoulder, sir, and it hurt.'

Mr Quinn came over and touched my shoulder. Then he leaned down and whispered to me to come with him. 'Just get on with it, the rest of you.'

Out in the corridor, he made me undo my shirt and show me what was inside. On totallysaints.com it tells you about Matt Talbot, who wore chains all the time. Obviously, I couldn't get any chains as such, so I'd stuffed my shirt with holly from the hermitage.

'Who did this?'

'Did it myself, sir.'

'You're cut. Take the holly out and I'll get some plasters.' When he was putting the plasters on, he said, 'I want you to come and see me at Home Time. I'm going to give you a letter to take to your dad. You're not in trouble, but it is important. OK?'

The letter was in a brown envelope. It was quite thick. Dad opened it as soon as I gave it to him. He read it and then put it in his pocket.

Anthony said, 'What's it about? Are they going on a trip?'

'No,' said Dad. 'Or. Yeah. Maybe. In a way. Eventually. Go and wash your hands.'

It was my turn to wash up and Anthony's to put away. Dad was supposed to be doing the floor, but when I came back into the dining room to make sure we hadn't missed any dishes, he was reading the letter again. He put it away as I came in, but I saw that one of the pages was yellow and it said 'Special Assessment'. I thought, 'Special', that's pretty good.

*

I think Dad must've stayed up late that night, because I fell asleep in my bed before he came upstairs to brush his teeth. In the middle of the night, I woke from a dream (which I don't want to talk about), got up and stretched out on the floor under the window again. It was really cold after the warm bed. I couldn't get to sleep. Suddenly I realized there was someone standing in the doorway. I thought, finally, a vision. But when it came closer, I could see it was just Dad. He bent down and picked me up, whispering, 'Shhhh, Damian. You've fallen out of bed. I'm just going to pop you back in. Don't wake up.'

I didn't like to tell him I was still awake. I just lay on my side so he wouldn't be able to see my face. I thought he'd go away then, but he didn't. He sat on the edge of the bed for a while. Then he tugged the collar of my pyjamas down at the shoulder. He was looking at the scratches. When he finally got up to go, I whispered, 'Dad, are you OK?'

'Are you awake?'

'Yes.'

'Go to sleep.'

'OK.'

'Damian . . .'

'Yeah?'

'What happened to your back?'

'Just some holly, you know.'

'Damian. Be good, won't you? Be really good.'

'That's what I'm trying to be. That's what I'm trying to be all the time.'

'I know it is, son. I know that.'

Then he went. After a while I heard the toilet flush. Then I got back on to the floor.

4

It's not as easy to be good as you might think. For instance, on the Monday the doorbell rang just after Dad had gone to work. Now, we're not supposed to answer the door when Dad isn't there. On the other hand, it was time to go to school. So it was a moral dilemma – answer the door (dis-obedient) and be on time for school (good), or don't answer the door (good) and be late for school (bad). Anthony doesn't think about these things. He just headed for the door, pulling his blazer on. I stopped him.

'Dad said not to answer the door.'

'It's twenty to,' he said. ' We're going to be late.'

Then whoever it was rang the doorbell again.

'But Dad said not to!' I was shouting now. It was making me panicky. 'Dad said not to do it and we're supposed to be being good!'

Anthony took a deep breath and said, 'OK. This is what we do. Get your bag. We'll leave for school. If there's someone outside, then they're just a coincidence. We're not answering the door. We're going to school. All right?'

'All right.' Anthony is very good at sorting out moral dilemmas when he tries.

The coincidence was a man in a white shirt with a *South Park* tie and a plastic name badge saying, 'Terry – IT'. 'I'm from that one there,' he said, and pointed at the house on the bend.

Anthony looked at the house. 'The corner position gives you extra garden, which is an asset, but you've no off-road parking, which is a definite disadvantage in this market.'

'Is your dad in?'

'Gone to work.'

'Your mum?'

'Dead,' said Anthony.

'Oh.'

Terry put his hands in his pockets, as though he was looking for something to give us. Anthony watched the pockets expectantly, but Terry didn't seem to be able to find anything.

'Can you give your dad a message?'

'Sure.'

'We haven't met. I leave for work before most people get up, but tell him if he wants to come over tonight, about seven o'clock, then cool. Most people will be there.'

'Can we come too?'

'Yeah. Sure. Hey, look at this.' He fiddled with his tie and it played the *South Park* theme tune, which was quite surprising.

'Who the hell is Terry?' Dad was getting agitated.

'Terry – IT over the road. He said to come at seven.'

'Come what for? A party? Supper? A game of Monopoly? Help him move a wardrobe?'

'He's got a tie that plays tunes and he said, "Cool." We think it's a party.'

'Meet-the-neighbours type of thing.'

'What time is it now? I'll have to go and get a bottle.'

'No need. We're baking a cake. Is that OK?'

'I'm surprised.'

'Surprised and pleased? Or surprised and disappointed?'

'Surprised and pleased that you've taken this opportunity to be excellent.'

It was my idea to bake the cake. When we got in from school, I'd said to Anthony, 'This is an opportunity to be excellent. Let's bake a cake.'

He was against it on the grounds that we didn't know how. But I remembered baking cakes loads of times in the past. It was one of the things I remembered a lot. Sometimes I even dreamed about it. I said, 'Put the oven on to 200°,' and we got cracking. We'd taken 110 grams of flour with 50 grams of margarine, two spoonfuls of water and a pinch of salt, mixed them and put them in the fridge to rest for twenty minutes, and that's as far as we'd got. The patron saint of bakers, by the way, is St Agatha of Catania (c 250).

Dad took the bag out of the fridge and said, 'This is brilliant, but it isn't cake. It's pastry.'

I realized then that my memory wasn't about cakes, it was about quiche. It's sad and worrying to think that you can forget bits of your favourite memory.

On the brighter side, pastry is more versatile than

cake, because you can make it into a tart. We made one using the apples we were supposed to eat after supper. We sliced and sugared them, fanned them out on the pastry base, put them in the oven and went to wash our hair. The smell of baking apples filled the house. We sat at the top of the stairs, just smelling it, while Dad sorted out our smart clothes. Luckily we'd worn them yesterday and they hadn't gone into the wash yet. Dad spruced them up with an iron and a sponge. He combed my hair, then stood back, looked at the two of us and went, 'Excellent. Truly excellent. Let's party!'

'Can we have a bit of the tart first? Or some toast? Anything? We're starving.'

'Hunger is the best sauce. There'll be food there.'

I carried the still-warm tart across the Close. Terry waved us in and took the pie off me.

Dad said, 'I've been hearing all about your tie.'

Terry made it play the tune again. We laughed, but the tune went on longer than the laugh and we all had to stand for a while listening to the tie.

'Well, that's all, folks,' said Terry when it finally finished. 'The others are in the living room.'

The others were four very clean men in white shirts and one bald tatty man in an old suit. They were all sitting in a circle, holding bits of paper. The tart was not in there and neither was any other food.

The man in the suit shook Dad's hand and said, 'Welcome to the Portland Meadows Homewatch. I'm your community police officer – Eddie. Obviously there is no community here yet, but you know what I mean. I'm here when you need me – whether it's for advice or help or just a cup of tea.'

Dad sat down and we sat on each side of him.

'I'll be honest with you – we've got Christmas coming up; these are new houses. Statistically, you are going to get done. When you do, you give me a call. I give you a crime number and you claim on your insurance.' And he handed round some little cards with his phone number on.

Anthony nudged me, pointed to his stomach, then his head, and made little scissory movements with his fingers. He was miming, 'My stomach thinks my throat is cut.' I knew, because my stomach was feeling the same way. To make matters worse, we could still smell the tart sitting out in the kitchen, all on its own.

Terry leaned forward. We leaned forward too. Maybe this was it. But instead of offering us food, he started on about his stereo. 'You see, this baby cost me close to three grand.' He pointed to a spaghetti of wires and cables sprawling around the room. 'I put it together myself. I spent ages deciding what to get, scoping out the best deals. That is part of me. If someone nicked that, I don't know what I'd do. It'd be like losing part of me. It'd be like a forced amputation. And the same with the computer, obviously. I mean, my memories are in there and my soul. If I lost that, it'd be like a bereavement. They're part of me, my belongings.'

He didn't mention any edible belongings.

'You can get an alarm or a dog,' said the community police officer. 'If you make it hard for them, they'll move on to the next house. In this case, your neighbour's house. Some of you might feel that that's a bit antisocial. I don't know.'

'Yeah, but I worked for this house, you know. This is me, this house. If I could—'

One of the very clean young men leaned forward and said, 'Isn't the problem here that our houses are built on sand?'

Dad sat up suddenly. 'Sand? They're not, are they? No, no. I was here when the footings were dug.'

The policeman said, 'I think we're talking metaphorically here, aren't we? It's in the Bible, isn't it – not building your house on sand, not putting your light under a bushel, all that.'

'That's right,' said the cleanest young man. 'Matthew, Chapter 7, Verse 26.'

'D'you mind me asking,' said the policeman, 'is the kettle actually on?'

Terry went out to the kitchen. While he was gone, the policeman said to the clean young men, 'So, at a guess, Mormons.'

'Latter-day Saints,' said one of the men. 'People call us Mormons, but we prefer Latter-day Saints. I'm Eli. This is Amos and that's John.'

This was exciting. 'You're saints!' I said.

'Latter-day Saints.'

'But saints, though.'

The community police officer started shuffling his papers and asked if there were any questions.

I put my hand up and asked, 'What exactly is a virgin martyr?'

Dad coughed and said, 'It's something they've been doing in school. Damian, why don't you go and help Terry in the kitchen. Anthony, you too.'

In the kitchen, Terry was spooning instant coffee into a mug. That's just one mug. The apple tart was on the side. We'd put cinnamon on it and some raisins. It smelt like a mixture of Christmas and summer. It was sitting on the side with no one bothering it. It was not going anywhere.

'Dad said we had to come and help you.'

'It's just a mug of coffee. There's nothing to do.'

It really was just one mug of coffee. My tummy made a noise almost as if it heard him. 'You could go and ask that copper if he takes sugar.'

Anthony didn't move. 'Our mum's dead. Did we tell you?'

'Yeah. Yeah, you did,' said Terry. This time he went for his cupboard. It was stuffed with big party packs of crisps. From somewhere underneath them, he pulled out two Penguins. He offered them to us, saying, 'Here, take these. Save them for home. I don't want crumbs on my carpet.'

On the way home, Anthony flashed his Penguin at me and said, 'Result. Told you. Works every time.'

I said, 'Are you sure it's completely honest?'

'She's completely dead, isn't she?'

Of course I knew that already, but no one had ever been so biological before.

When Dad caught up with us he said, 'You two were great tonight. I'm going to buy you anything you want from the chippy.'

Anthony wanted spring rolls and then chicken in black bean sauce. Somehow I wasn't hungry. Even when Dad took me inside the chippy and showed me the menu, nothing really caught my fancy. I wasn't hungry any more.

When we got home, Dad and Anthony started to eat their food straight from the polystyrene trays. I went and got plates and knives and forks.

'Damian, don't bother. It's late. We don't want to be clearing up. Here, have some rice.'

I just carried on setting the table.

'Damian . . .'

'We've got to do things properly. That's the point.'

'What point?'

'You said we've got to do things properly. We've got to be excellent. You said. And now you're eating out of the trays. We didn't used to do that before.' I was shouting now. 'Sit at the table!'

Dad tried to calm me down. 'Damian, you think you're upset, but really you're just hungry.'

'I'm not hungry. I just want us to sit at the table like a proper family. And do things right.'

'I will if you eat a bit – like a proper family.'

'OK, then.'

Dad came and sat at the table and gave me some chow mein.

Anthony said, 'Why can't you just act normal?'

Dad said, 'Things aren't normal, are they? So how can we act normal?' And he took one of Anthony's spring rolls and gave it to me.

It was horrible. It had cabbage in instead of bean sprouts. But it made me feel a bit better.

I think it was the spring roll that stopped me sleeping properly. I kept waking up from these dreams (which I don't want to talk about). I even got back into bed after a while to see if being comfortable made a difference, but it didn't. As soon as it was light, I sneaked off down to the hermitage.

When I looked inside, there was someone there – a tall, bony woman with bright blue eyes. I knew who it was right away. I said, 'St Clare of Assisi (1194–1253).'

She smiled and said, 'Is right.' She looked around. 'I like a hermitage. Had one myself once.'

'I know.'

'Used to go and hide myself away up there. Anyone needed me, I'd send them a vision. Sort them out.'

'Be good to be able to do that. I could stay here and send a vision of myself to school.'

'It's a skill not everyone has. I was unusual. I was like human television. That's why I'm the patron saint of television. For my sins. Well, for my virtues, shall we say? You see all sorts on there now. Mind you, nothing shocks me any more. Keeps me busy, though. That's why I like a hermitage.'

'Our house seemed a bit, you know, inappropriate. Compared to St Simeon's column or St Ursula and her 11,000 holy companions.'

She gave a snort. 'The 11,000 holy companions are a mistake in the translation. I wouldn't let them keep you awake at night. There were only ever eleven of them, if the truth be told.'

'But there are thousands of people up there with you?'

'Tens of thousands. Dozens of thousands. Hundreds of thousands. Millions even.'

'Only I did wonder if you'd ever come across a St Maureen?'

She thought for a while. But the answer was no. Then again, as she said, it is infinite up there. 'Absolutely infinite. In my Father's house are many mansions. John, Chapter 14.'

I said, 'Verse 2.'

She said, 'Is right.' And then she was gone.

Given the choice, I wouldn't have picked St Clare for my first vision. But obviously she's a good saint and she was very interesting to talk to. And any kind of vision is exciting. So, to be philosophical about it, it made me happy.

5

One of the big changes that has happened to women since the Middle Ages is skin care. St Clare had very dry skin, with little red veins in her cheeks. My mum used to wear a tinted moisturizer. It nourished her skin and it provided a good, light base for make-up. She worked on the Clinique counter in Kendal's, in Manchester. Part of her job was to look more beautiful than normal mothers. She used to wait for us at the school gates. When we got home she used to take the moisturizer off with a piece of cotton wool. She used to call it 'peeling her face'. Anyway, one day she wasn't at the school gates at Home Time. We waited and waited and Mrs Deus, the secretary, phoned one of the normal mothers, who came and took us back to her house instead. After a while, Dad came to collect us and he kept saying thank you and also, 'She's in the best place.'

We went with Dad to the best place and, to be honest, I couldn't see what was good about it. Mum was not allowed out of bed. The telly was on all the time and everyone looked miserable. Mum stayed there for weeks and weeks and she looked more miserable every time we saw her. Her skin went grey and dry like St Clare's. She even had the little veins in her cheeks. In fact that's where I first became interested in saints. There was a lot of talk about saints at the time. Some of the doctors were saints. Some of the nurses were angels. St Rita – patron saint of wives – she was mentioned a lot. St Joseph – patron saint of the chronically ill – there was a card with him on it stuck to the bedstead. And our school at the time was 'All Saints Primary', which was helpful.

When the three of us were at home, on our own, I used to look them up on Google. That's how I found totallysaints.com. It was good to read about all the miracles they did and to think that things did not always turn out the way you expected. And then one day someone said she'd gone to a better place. Which only went to show that the best place couldn't have been the best place after all, not if there was somewhere better. No one ever took us to the better place, though, and when we made inquiries, no one was very geographical about it. They just said, 'She's gone to a better place and now you have to be really, really, good boys for your dad.' They seemed to be hinting that he might go off to the better place himself if we weren't careful. So we were careful. Always. All the time.

I definitely remember someone saying we would see her again in the better place. So when the talk of Cromarty Close started I thought, This must be the better place. Otherwise, why go there? The minute I saw those pointy roofs I knew I'd made a mistake. It was good but not that good.

It turned out that when people were talking about the better place, they were just being metaphorical.

6

The next day, Dad stopped me on the way out to school. 'You remember the trip you had the letter about? It's today.'

'Oh. But won't we be too late?' When we went to Llangollen with All Saints Primary we had to be there at half past seven.

'No, no. It's not the whole class. It's just you and me. Come on, jump in.'

So I got in the car and off we went. I don't usually ride in the front passenger seat, but because it was just me and Dad I did that day. It was good. He gave me a little photocopied map with a yellow highlighter ring drawn round one of the roads.

He said, 'Keep that handy till I need it.' It all seemed a bit unusual, but before I could ask him a question, he said, 'Here. Look what I found. We haven't listened to this for ages,' and he put on a tape of Martin Jarvis reading *Just William*. It was really funny – the one about the baby with lumbago. I laughed so much that I didn't notice till we got there that Dad wasn't listening. Still, he was going somewhere he'd never been before, so I imagine he was concentrating on directions.

We parked outside a big old house in a wide, curvy road at the edge of a park.

'What is it?'

'It's just a house.'

We were at the door. There was a brass nameplate.

'Why's it called Huskisson House? Are the people called Huskisson?'

'I don't know. I don't know the people.'

'Then what are we doing here?' I started to get one of my panics. I said, 'I really have been trying to be good, you know.'

'I know. And you are good. Very good. Excellent. I want them to see how excellent you are.'

We went into a room with a wicker chair. There was a pile of magazines on the table – *Scottish Caravanner* was the most interesting-looking one. A woman with long straight hair and long straight earrings came and asked us to follow her. I realized when we got to the corridor that I'd accidentally brought the magazine with me. I didn't want them to think I was stealing it, so I went to replace it. When I got back out into the corridor, there was no one there. I was under a great temptation to just walk out of the main entrance and run away, but then Dad looked out of one of the doors and called me in.

When I went into the room, the woman with the long earrings was saying, 'And he's been self-harming?'

'Well, he's got some scratches.'

'Shall we take a look, then? Damian, would you mind taking your shirt off.'

I took my shirt off and she looked at my back and I looked at this big sad mask she had on the wall. I think it was African.

She said, 'Not very deep but lots of them. What did he do them with?'

Dad looked at me.

I said truthfully, 'Holly.'

'So you did this yourself?'

'Well . . . I put the holly in my shirt.'

Dad said, 'Why?'

But before I could explain she raised a finger and said, 'I want to avoid anything confrontational.' She asked me lots more questions. She asked me how I got to sleep at night. If I had bad dreams at all. The strangest one was, 'Do you see things that aren't there?'

'If you can see something, then it's there, isn't it? How can it not be there if you can see it?'

'We'll come back to that,' she said with a big, bright smile. Then she took one of her earrings out and started to fiddle with it. 'I'm going to say a few words and I'd like you to tell me the first word that my word puts into your head. Do you think you could do that for me?'

It didn't sound very difficult.

'All right, then. And the first word is little.'

'Flower.'

'OK.' She looked a bit puzzled and she wrote something down, saying, 'Interesting. Unusual.'

I said, 'Like the Little Flower, you know.'

'No need to explain. Just the first word you think of. The next word is cake.'

'Soap.'

'Very good. Bell.'

'Leper.'

She frowned and said, 'Oh', but then she said, 'Kay' a bit later.

'Shirt.'

'Hair.'

She didn't say OK this time. She said, 'Excuse me?'

Dad said, 'Hair shirt, you know, like . . .'

She flapped her hand at him but kept looking at me. 'Fly,' she said.

I said, 'Joseph of Copertino (1603–63).' I could see this didn't mean anything to her, so I went on, 'He was a monk. He was supposed to be not right in the head, but he could levitate. When they were building the church at Grottella he used to fly up to the roof to help the workmen. I know it sounds mad, but all sorts of people saw him, including the famous cynic Voltaire and the great mathematician Leibniz. It's illuminating to think of Leibniz – one of the greatest minds in history – being awestruck by a supposed simpleton.'

I think she was impressed, because she dropped her earring. Also she didn't ask me any more words. That one must have just hit the spot.

Dad said, 'I don't know where he gets it.'

I said, 'Totallysaints.com. It has great links and you can search for saints by what they're patron of. Say you wanted to know who was the patron saint of African masks . . .'

She said, 'I don't. It's not mine.' And closed her notebook, picked her earring up and put it back in.

On the way to school, I could see Dad was worried about something, so I decided to make conversation. I said, 'It would probably be one of the martyrs of Uganda. They're the most popular African saints. The main one was beheaded, but the rest were—'

'Damian, will you please, for once, shut up about saints. In fact, not for once, for good. OK? It's not . . . natural. It's not excellent. OK?'

'What!' I was astounded that he could say something like that. 'How can they not be excellent? That's the whole point of them. The whole point is—'

'Damian, I'm warning you.'

I decided to forbear. I changed the subject to Scottish caravans and camper vans. There are two different sorts of caravan – tourers and statics. Statics don't move. Tourers have names like Marauder and Ambassador and Highwayman. 'Why, though? I mean, you can't really see a highwayman driving round in a camper van, can you? Or an ambassador. Unless he was the ambassador of a very, very small country.'

Dad looked like he wasn't really interested, but he must have been quite interested in these observations because he did stop and buy me a king-size Mars bar. 'Here, get your choppers round that,' he said.

At Home Time I tried to describe it all to Anthony. 'I kept trying to be good,' I said, 'but I couldn't figure out what they wanted.'

Anthony said, 'They think you're bonkers.'

I'd never thought of that. But the thing is, so what? They thought Joseph of Copertino was bonkers and he could fly. He could even fly away if he wanted to. Miles away.

It was getting dark when we got back to ours. The Latter-day Saints passed us on their bikes. They all had reflective strips on their helmets. They glowed like little haloes. When we went to bed, I kept thinking about them and how good it would be if they were saints literally. But then I started to worry about what the latter-day bit meant.

Dad was addicted to worldly knowledge. In our old house he belonged to a pub-quiz team called

'The Know-Alls'. They always won. He used to wake us up and say, 'Which sport do you win by going backwards?' and so on. So I decided to go and ask him what latter-day meant. I admit it was three o'clock in the morning, but I was still surprised when he said, 'I don't know, do I?' and rolled over and went to sleep. I climbed in next to him. He doesn't have the general knowledge he once had.

In the end, I couldn't get back to sleep. I decided to go and Google something – the Mormons. I eventually found latterdaysaints.org, which told me all I needed to know. The Latter-day Saints or Mormons were founded in New York in 1827 by a man called Joseph Smith. An angel called Moroni gave him a set of gold tablets covered in strange writing. He found that if he wore a special pair of spectacles he could read the writing and that it told the story of how the lost tribe of Israel went to live in America in 600 BC. The angel took the gold plates and the spectacles back when Mr Smith had finished reading. It was all a bit literal.

It was still dark, but I decided to put my uniform on and go down to the hermitage. As soon as I stepped outside, I changed my mind. It was freezing, like stepping into a cold shower when you think it's warm. I suddenly realized what a great idea bed was. Unfortunately, the front door had closed behind me and I couldn't get back in.

It wasn't any warmer in the hermitage. I began to regret putting windows in. I huddled in the corner and tried to take my mind off the cold by putting some of the tinted moisturizer on the back of my hand. It wasn't the colour of her skin but it was the colour that her skin was, if you see what I mean. Then I tried to meditate on the difficulties of being good. You think you're being good, then it turns out you're being a problem or not natural. Then I started to think about the saints and how Dad didn't seem to like them any more and maybe they weren't all they were cracked up to be and it was just all a big misunderstanding. Then I thought that these doubts were just another temptation, so I tried to say a prayer, but all I could think of to say was, 'In the name of the Father and of the Son and of the Holy Spirit, Amen. My Mum is Dead. Amen.'

Even that little prayer took me about five minutes to say because my teeth kept chattering. God must have heard me, though, because he answered it. And you know what? He did the same thing as everyone else. He gave me something.

Just as I finished the prayer a train went past. A huge gust of oily air burst into the hermitage, making all the flaps flap. I looked out. The train had no windows. It was just a huge block of night on wheels, screaming past the holly bushes.

As I watched, a little scrap of darkness seemed to get free of the big darkness and come rolling through the air towards me. It crashed into the front end of the hermitage, smashing the boxes flat and letting even more cold air in. It squatted on the flattened cardboard like a big leathery toad.

I went over and touched it. It was a bag. It had come apart along the zip and its insides were spilling out. And its insides were money. It wasn't a vision or a visitation as such. I suppose you could call it a sign. A big loud sign. It was money. Banknotes. Piles and piles of them. Thousands and thousands of pounds. Millions, even.

7

For the record, this wasn't the first time in history that money fell down out of the sky. For instance, in Turkey, in the second century, if a girl was getting married her father had to give the husband some money called a dowry. There were three girls who just didn't have any money, so their father was going to sell their honour, which you could do in those days. Anyway, one night St Nicholas of Myra climbed up on the roof, dropped three bags of money down the chimney – one for each girl – and so saved their honour. He started being saintly when very young. For instance, he refused to breastfeed every Friday because he was fasting.

He's the patron saint of sailors, pawnbrokers, unmarried girls, children (because of a bizarre incident with some boys who were trapped in a pickle barrel) and people who sell perfume. Now he's Santa Claus as well. He's probably the most successful saint.

When the bag of money landed in front of me, it put me in mind of St Nicholas straight away. I could have asked him for guidance. Or I could have asked St Matthew, who is the patron saint of money. Or I could have called the police. Or my dad.

Personally, I ran across the field shouting, 'Anthony! Anthony! Come and look at this!' I was that excited, you see.

I'm not sure now that it was the best idea.

When I got to the house, it was still dark but there was a light on in the kitchen and I could see Anthony making toast. I tapped on the window. He jumped in fright, but then he saw who it was and let me in.

'What are you doing out there? You're freezing. Where've you been? Have you been out all night?'

My teeth were still chattering. I said, 'I've found . . . I've found . . .'

'What?'

'Come and look.'

Anthony put his coat on. He could tell I was excited, but he wasn't that convinced. 'This had better be something that other people can see.'

This reminded me of what the woman had said at Huskisson House. What if you could see things that weren't there? What if it wasn't as optical as I thought it was? But when we got to the hermitage, the bag was there. I pointed to it.

Anthony said, 'What?'

'You know when you tell people Mum is dead and they give you stuff?'

He nodded.

'Well, I told God.'

I pulled back the box and Anthony saw it – a big bag stuffed with money. His face glowed. He says now that it's still the most beautiful thing he's ever seen. He was so happy just then.

'And it's from God, you reckon?'

I nodded.

'Well, he really wanted to cheer us up.'

It needed the two of us to carry the money back across the field towards the house. Think of that. More money than we could carry. I wanted to spread it all out on the dining table so Dad would see it when he got home and be of good cheer, but Anthony said we mustn't tell Dad about it.

'Why not?'

'Tax.'

I had to ask him what tax was.

'If Dad knew about it, he'd have to tell the government, and if they knew about it, they'd want to tax it. At 40 per cent – that's nearly half of it. We should just hide it and go to school.'

But we couldn't. We had to know how much was there. We tipped the money on to the table.

'Anyway,' Anthony said, 'if God had wanted Dad to have this, he would've sent him a cheque in the post.'

It was hard to argue with that.

I started to help him count. At first we just tried to count all the tenners using our ten times table, but we lost track of which ones we'd counted. The room seemed to be filling up with notes. Then Anthony had the idea of counting them into piles of a hundred, and then counting the hundreds. But even that was no good. After ten minutes the whole floor was tiled with wads of money. We couldn't find anywhere to sit, let alone count. So then we tried making them into piles of a thousand. There were 229 piles of a thousand. Plus 370 pounds change.

That's 229,370 pounds. Or twenty-two million, 937 thousand pence.

For a while we just looked at it. Then Anthony picked up a thousand pounds and put it crossways on top of another thousand. Then he picked up another and put it crossways on top of that. Then I picked up a pile and put that on top of the other three. Then Anthony. Then me, and on and on, building a tower of cash. We got it almost as tall as me before it fell over. Then we both started laughing.

That was the first time we played Cash Jenga. We played it every night for the next week. The highest we ever got was Anthony's eyebrows. But that first time was the best, when it just sort of invented itself out of our excitement.

Cash Jenga is a great game if you can afford it.

We were late for school, but somehow it didn't matter. Whenever we saw each other in the play-ground or in the corridor, we just grinned. Having a secret is like having a pair of wings tucked in under your blazer. I gave Barry my Pringles (barbecue flavour) without being asked. I just handed them to him while we were lining up at the end of Small Play. I said, 'Enjoy.' He looked a bit surprised.

*

On the way home, we stopped at the shop and Anthony bought a bottle of Sunny Delight the size of an oxygen tank. He saw me looking at it and said to the man, 'Make it a double.'

While the man was getting my bottle, a girl from Anthony's class – the one with the nice corn rows in her hair – came in and Anthony said, 'Make it three and have something for yourself.' And he gave a tenner to the man and the bottle to the girl. Just as he was handing it to her, Barry came in and went, 'Ooooohooo, you love her! You bought her Sunny Delight.'

'Why shouldn't I buy her Sunny Delight?'

'Why shouldn't you buy *me* Sunny Delight?'

'All right, then, I will.'

So he bought another bottle. By which time, Barry's mate Kaloo was there saying, 'You only bought that cos you're scared of Barry.'

So Anthony bought a fifth bottle and gave that to Kaloo.

By now people were piling in to see what was going on. Kaloo went, 'The new kid's sucking up to us. Buying us Sunny Delight.'

'I'm not sucking up to anyone,' said Anthony, and he proved it by buying everyone a bottle. Twenty-three bottles of Sunny Delight and a box of

Walker's prawn cocktail. Not a packet, a box. One of the big boxes you get from the wholesaler.

'Spending money like it's going out of fashion,' said the shopkeeper.

'It is going out of fashion,' said Anthony.

Outside, on the pavement, everyone scrummed hungrily round the Walker's box. A couple of them left their bikes sprawled on the pavement. Anthony shouted, 'Who wants to lend us a bike?'

A couple of lads stood up and looked at him.

'Tenner,' offered Anthony.

The bike owners clambered over each other to get to us first. In the end, we went for Terry Keegan's Raleigh Max and Franny Amoo's Pavement Shark. Payment was on collection of the bikes from our house, before five, which is when Dad was due home.

It was good to be able to get nice stuff without having to go on about dead people. Both the Pavement Shark and the Raleigh Max have excellent suspension, so we rolled home over the back field, by the railway. Anthony talked about all the things we could get – bikes of our own, quad bikes even, new trainers, new tops, mobiles, Beyblades. All the things that Dad said were a waste of money – sea monkeys, or the X-Box, or the Gamecube, or extra channels or X-ray specs.

'They don't work. You only see skeletons.'

'Skeletons are good.'

And when we got home, instead of turning the oven on, we called Pizza Reaction and ordered pizzas. I asked for one with extra cheese and extra pepperoni. While we were waiting we played Cash Jenga, which I won.

Then Anthony thought of real-money Monopoly. 'It'll be brilliant,' he said. 'I'll be banker.' But we'd only just got the board set up when Mr Pizza Reaction came up on his moped.

As we opened the door, Dad was just pulling into the car port. 'What the hell is going on?' he asked, as he headed for the house.

'We've ordered pizzas instead of cooking. We thought it would be excellent.'

'Where did you get the money?'

'I've got money,' said Anthony.

'What, from your birthday and stuff?'

'Stuff, yeah. It's sterling, so we have to spend it before Day anyway. We ordered one for you.'

'What kind of one?'

'Seafood with extra anchovies.'

Anthony opened the box and steam curled out like candle smoke and the smell of cooked cheese and damp bread filled the room.

'Nice. That is very, very nice of you.' Dad just stared at the pizza for the longest time, saying nothing.

'Is it the wrong kind?' I asked.

He suddenly marched into the kitchen, blew his nose and came back saying, 'It's the right kind. It's just the right kind. It's very much the right kind.'

I said, 'Cardboard boxes are definitely better than the polystyrene ones. The polystyrene ones make them go rubbery, I think.'

'Yes, they do,' said Dad. His eyes were so shiny that I thought for a minute he was going to cry. Obviously people don't cry about pizza. 'You're very good lads,' he said. And then he picked up the biggest slice of pizza I'd ever seen, folded it over and put the end in his mouth. He looked like a gorilla gargoyle and we all laughed.

I said, 'Who invented pizza?' I didn't really want to know. I just thought Dad might like to talk about general knowledge, the way he used to. I remember him reading a whole book on the history of the potato.

'Pizza,' he said, 'was invented in Naples. It was originally just a herby bread which market traders used to sell to poor people. When Queen Margherita came to visit Naples in 1889, she really took to it, so she got the most famous pizza maker – Rafaelle Esposito – to make one specially for her. It was his idea to put basil, tomato and mozzarella on top. Green basil, red tomatoes and white cheese, you see, colours of the Italian flag. And that's why it's called Pizza Margherita.'

We all cleared up and that was a great day.

8

Anthony says I need to get more financial about the story. So, financially, we had 229,370 pounds sterling. On the morning of 1 December this was worth 323,056 euros. It's true that you can't buy love or happiness with money, but it is interesting to see what you can buy.

For instance, you could buy 15,390 pairs of Micro Turbo racers at 20.99 a pair. Or 3,756 Sky Patrol quick-charge, easy-to-fly remote-control helicopters at 85.99 each. Or 22,937 Airzookas (they fire balls of air at people). Or 43,159 kite-in-a-keyring sets. Or 5,736 table-top candyfloss makers. Or 1,434 Shogun Nude BMXs. Or 2,699 Gameboy Advance Sps.

On 1 December we had seventeen days left to spend it.

On the same morning, we opened the front door to find six lads and two girls waiting on their bikes. As soon as Anthony looked out, they all started shouting, 'Want a bike? Anthony, want a bike? Anthony? Anthony, have a bike!'

Anthony took a good look at each bike. 'I think what we'd really like is a lift,' he said. 'Kaloo and Tricia.'

Kaloo McLoughlin and Tricia Springer had BMXs – the kind with the little pommels sticking out of the back axle for you to stand on. Anthony went on Kaloo's bike and I went on Tricia's. We cruised to school with all the other bikes trailing along after us like a motorcade. Everyone was looking at us. It was the best thing. At the gates, Anthony gave Kaloo and Tricia a tenner each.

Tricia didn't seem that happy about it. 'It's a kilometre. A tenner's too much. I just want enough to buy a set of glitter pens.'

The truth is, we didn't have anything smaller than a tenner. If you asked our Anthony now, he'd say this was where everything started to go wrong.

According to him, the problem with the money supply created an inflationary environment in the playground. We didn't even know we had a problem then, though. We just thought we had over 229,000 pounds to spend.

It seemed like it would be easy. At lunch, for instance, we had Hot Dinners instead of sandwiches and we didn't have to queue. Peter Ahenacho queued for us and brought it over to the table, like a waiter. Tracey Edwards went and got our cutlery and drinks and cleared up after us. We gave them ten pounds each. Afterwards, we had extra helpings of pudding (chocolate flan) for ten pounds each. We were just finishing when Barry came and sat at our table. He had a set of walkie-talkie watches.

'They've got a 200-metre radius. New batteries. Matching designer fascias. What d'you think?'

'Ten quid,' said Anthony.

'No way! You gave her ten quid for fetching a fork. Forty.'

'Forty quid, then.'

So we'd spent 100 quid today already.

Out on the playground other people came up to us with stuff they'd brought in from home. There was a Gameboy; some goggles that helped you see at night, half a dozen micro-machines. We spent 150 pounds just walking from the monkey bars to the boys' toilets.

In the boys' toilets, there was a boy from Year Five called Aamar. He had a big faded yellow box with footballers on the front. The corners of the box were all blunt. 'Subbuteo, that's what this is. You must've heard of it. It's a legend.'

No, we hadn't.

'Football game, man. Classic, isn't it? This is my dad's from way back. Family heirloom.'

'So it's second-hand, then?'

'Not second-hand, man, antique. Antique. Legend. Timeless. Look. These are the teams – Arsenal and Man City.'

He opened the lid. There were dozens of tiny players lying in rows like they were asleep. It had miniature floodlights, ambulances, referees, linesmen, managers' dugouts, a TV van, advertising hoardings. Everything. It was a world, where you could be in charge. We had to have it.

'Forty quid.'

'Forty! You're jesting, my friend. You'd give me ten quid if I sharpened your pencil, mate. I'm looking for a ton for this.'

'A hundred quid! Now who's jesting? I could

buy a real team for a hundred quid. I could buy Crewe Alexandra.'

'Do it, then. It won't have managers.' He pulled a freezer bag from his pocket. Inside it were two tiny plastic men in sheepskin coats. One of them had a little hat on. The other had his collar up. We both gasped. 'It will not disappoint you, my friend.'

I said, 'How are we going to get all this stuff home?'

Anthony said, 'A hundred quid for this but you deliver.'

Aamar spat on his hand and held it out for Anthony. Anthony looked at the hand and passed him a paper towel.

It was all a bit unenlightening.

Outside the gates after school, everyone who had a bike was waiting for us, shouting, 'Want a lift? Give you a lift?'

We breezed past them out of the gates, where a big black saloon was waiting. Anthony had booked us a taxi. We climbed in and waved goodbye.

I said, 'That was a great day. If we go on like that, we'll spend the money in no time.'

'Keep your voice down,' hissed Anthony. He nodded towards the cab driver, then whispered,

'We've spent a bit yesterday and 350 quid today, which leaves us about 229,000. If we spent this much every day it would take us 655 days to get rid of the money.'

'Oh.'

'We've got sixteen days after today. Mind you, we haven't paid for the taxi yet.' The taxi was four quid all the way home, which is actually cheaper than second helpings of pudding when you think about it. Anthony gave the man a tenner and told him to keep the change. Which was a mistake really, as it would've been good to start getting some change.

9

The minute we arrived at school next morning, we were surrounded by people trying to sell us stuff. Anthony bought: two micro-scooters (boxed); a Real Madrid away shirt; an original Harry Potter swatch watch; a video tape of *The Blair Witch Project* (someone said if you watched it you died, so we never did); a proper casey signed by the actual treble-winning Man United team; a packet of space ice cream; a pen that writes under water and a digital camera disguised as a pen (we didn't have the right kind of computer to get the pictures off it).

People tried to sell us rubbish as well – for instance, those toys you get in Happy Meals or the

Make Your Own Crystal Garden set which five different people tried to sell me and which no one ever tried to make. But it didn't matter. If we said no, someone else could buy it. Everyone had money now because nearly everyone had sold something to us. There was money everywhere. Money was a craze, like yakky yo-yos or Beyblades. Football was out. The playground was one big car-boot sale.

Mr Quinn came over to me and said, 'Lots of excitement on the playground today, Damian.'

I said, 'It's all very unenlightening.'

He looked at me a bit strangely.

Anthony wanted to buy some flying saucers on the way home but when we got to the shop, the shelves were almost empty. They'd bought everything except the Fisherman's Friends and Vim.

The shop man said, 'What's going on? Where's it all come from?'

Anthony decided we shouldn't go there any more just in case.

I didn't buy anything much personally, though I did manage to get to the repository shop at the back of St Margaret Mary's. I got statues of St Francis, St Martin de Porres, the Little Flower, Gerard Majella and the Child of Prague. I got miraculous medals of

St Benedict, St Bernadette and St Anthony. They had a St Christopher, but I don't count him as a proper saint personally. They had colourful cards of all the above plus St Michael the Archangel with a burning sword. They all fitted on my windowsill. It was a different matter with the micro-scooters and the Airzooka. Anthony tried to squeeze everything under the bed, but there was hardly any space because of the Subbuteo and the money.

'You'll have to put them in your den.'

'It's not a den, it's a hermitage, and I don't want it cluttered up with worldly goods. That's the whole point.'

'You know what we could do? We could rent a garage, a lock-up.'

'I don't know why we don't just tell Dad. What's the point in having all this stuff if we can't even play with it?'

'OK. OK. OK. We'll play Subbuteo.'

He didn't actually want to play. He was just making a point. We spread the cloth out on the floor and it was so green, it was like having a real little lawn in your room. You flick the player with your finger and the player flicks the ball. Sometimes you miss the ball and then it's the other one's turn. Anthony could hit the ball five or six times in a row and I'd move the linesmen up and down the touchline. We barely spoke as we played and the cloth seemed to grow bigger and greener, so it was like being on a real pitch, except it was quiet and everyone did what you told them to. Anthony flicked one in from the wing that dropped into the centre. There was nothing between him and my goal. You're allowed to move your goalie while the other one takes his kick. He shot. I quickly moved my St Gerard Majella statue into the goal. The ball hit the skull at St Gerard's feet and went bouncing off down the pitch, into Anthony's area.

'What the hell was that supposed to be?'

'I prayed.'

'You can't pray in football.'

'Excuse me. Brazilians pray all the time. They're always crossing themselves.'

'Saints do not come down and kick the ball for them.'

'How d'you know? They always win.'

'If you can have a saint, I can have Action Man.'

So Anthony laid his Action Man across the mouth of the goal.

'What? Where's the logic in that? You can pray to a saint. You can't pray to a doll.'

'Action Man is not a doll.'

'A doll is a doll is a doll and Action Man, I hate to tell you, is a doll.'

'It's got a grappling hook.'

'Barbie with a grappling hook.'

'What're you talking about, Barbie? It's a bloke. It's got grip-action hands.'

'St Francis could talk to animals.'

'Dr stupid Dolittle can talk to animals. Are you going to play him out on the left?'

We were so absorbed in this discussion that we didn't hear anyone coming upstairs or opening the door until it was too late. Until Dad was looking down at the Subbuteo, saying, 'Where the hell did that come from?'

Anthony can lie so fast it feels like the truth but blurred. 'Won it,' he said.

'Won it for what?'

'Art.' He was actually picking up speed. He was amazing.

'Art? What did you do? Paint the Sistine Chapel?'

'Made a model.'

'What of?'

'You know. What's it called? Tracy Island. It's excellent. The best.'

'Excellent. The best.' Dad said the words slowly to himself, as though they were his favourite flavour. He was lost. That's the other thing about Anthony's lies. They weren't just quick, they were tasty. People wanted to swallow them.

Dad looked at me. I did a St Roch. There's no patron saint of lying. You tell a lie; you're on your own.

To be nautical about this, we were getting into murky waters. The first chance I got, I retreated to the hermitage to contemplate my situation. I took St Francis with me, to help me focus. Unfortunately, Anthony had got there first. The place was cluttered up with material possessions, namely the two micro-scooters (boxed) and the Airzooka. There was no chance of a visitation as long as they were there.

I went and got the tartan blanket that used to be in the boot of the car and covered them up with it so that it looked like a couch. It was better than looking like a shop window. I stood the statue of St Francis up on the back of it, looking down at me. It was one of those of him holding a bird's nest. The minute I put it down, I had my idea.

I got a wad of money from the bag under the bed, remembering to zip it tight afterwards and to push the Subbuteo back in front of it. Then I took the money down to the Shopping City. Just as you go in, there's a place that used to be a swimming pool but now it's a pet shop. There's a massive cat fish in the baby pool and the main pool is ornamental carp. If you dip your fingers in the water, the fish come up and let you stroke their heads. The staff say it's because they're friendly. It could be because they want to get out of there, though. You can't tell with fish.

All around the poolside, where the changing lockers used to be, that's where they keep the birds. Hundreds and hundreds of them piled up on top of each other in little cages. It's very noisy, not because of singing, but because of wings buzzing like pages in a flicker book. I asked the bloke if I could buy some.

'Sure. What d'you want? Zebra finches . . .'
'Yeah.'
'Our canaries are going cheep. Ha ha.'
'I'll have some of them as well, then.'

'We do have parakeets and cockatiels, that type of thing.'

'They sound good too.'

'You'll have to make your mind up.'

But the nice thing about being rich is that you don't have to make your mind up. 'I was thinking of having some of each.' He looked none too certain, so I showed him my money and then he looked worse. I said, 'It was given me, after my mum died.'

So he took me round with a shopping trolley. When you choose a bird, they put it in a little box, a bit like a cake box with holes in. I tried to pick one from each cage. It was hard to choose, but I asked for guidance and did my best, and after one trip round the poolside I had two dozen boxes of birds and no cash left.

The man helped me push the trolley to the door. 'You'll have to bring that back, you know. How're you getting home?'

'Oh, I'm not going far. I'll bring the trolley back right away.'

I pushed the trolley over the road and took the path up the Rise. When I got to the top, I lined up all the boxes. I opened the first one, then the next. Nothing happened. You have to tip the box a bit when you open it. If you do, the birds inside fan their wings, lift their necks and fly off. I opened the next box and tipped it, and the next, and the next. Birds exploded from the boxes like fireworks. Parakeets went off like rockets. Zebra finches went up like showers of sparks. The cockatiels screamed as they whirled away into the sky, flying round and round each other. The whole sky was full of colours and singing.

In case you don't know, this is what St Francis did when he was my age (i.e. in 1190). He bought some birds from the market and let them go. So I was actually doing a saintish thing. In fact St Francis didn't have a shopping trolley, so he probably didn't do it to as many birds as me. So technically I was being more saintly than him even. The parakeets flew low over my head, like they were trying to thank me. Their long red tails streamed out behind them like fire.

I turned around to watch them and there was a man behind me, in a tatty brown gown, with a bald head and a big hole in the back of each hand. 'Well,' he said, 'this brings back memories.'

I said, 'St Francis of Assisi (1181–1226)?'

'I did this, you know.'

'I know. I know. That's why I did it.'

'Course, mine was mainly pigeons and songbirds. We couldn't source the tropicals back then, or the fancies really.'

'Do you know of a St Maureen at all?'

'Doesn't ring a bell to be honest.'

'Oh.'

'But there again, I'm kept very busy these days. My trouble is I've become increasingly relevant as time's gone by. There's the environment, animal rights, the Third World, and now this whole Muslim thing. I met the Sultan, you know.'

'I know. In Acre in 1219. You walked over hot coals without being hurt.'

'Don't try that at home.'

The parakeets came swooping back and flew over our heads towards town. We strolled up after them. You could see the whole muddy river now, and the town perched on the edge of it and the oil refinery with its plumes of bright yellow smoke. And the Widnes–Runcorn bridge like a big stepladder leading up to Heaven.

'I was the first vernacular poet in Europe. And the first environmentalist. And I started out by doing exactly what you're doing. Setting birds free.'

'What did you do after that?'

'Well, you know . . .' He waved his hand towards the Shopping City. There was a bus pulling up and crowds of people waiting to get on it. 'I helped the poor.'

'Of course. Of course you did. That's brilliant. Thanks.'

I ran all the way home.

10

The Widnes–Runcorn two-hinged arch bridge – proper name 'the Jubilee Bridge' – was built in 1961. It's not really a ladder to Heaven. This doesn't mean there's no such thing as a ladder to Heaven. There is. It's in Genesis, Chapter 28, Verse 12.

Every time you do a good deed, it takes you up a rung. Well, 229,000 pounds is enough money to give 458 poor people 500 pounds each, and 458 good deeds equals 458 rungs of the ladder, which is a long way up. We would be practically saints in Heaven by the time we'd given it all away. I decided to tell Anthony about the exciting opportunity for canonization.

He was behind the telly, rigging up a new Digibox. 'Anthony,' I said, 'do you ever feel that the money is hollow and meaningless?'

'How can it be meaningless? It means we're rich.'

'What has it given us really, apart from piles of stuff?'

He switched the telly on and flicked through all the channels, making sure the new ones were there, and said, 'Thirty new channels, that's what.' Then he sat down to watch *World Federation Monster Truck Tug of War*.

'Won't Dad notice thirty extra channels on his telly?'

'Dad never notices anything.'

The Monster Trucks were good but not mean- ingful. 'Imagine if we could be saints.'

'Why?'

'I think we should give the money to the poor. We've got enough to give 458 poor people 500 pounds each. And then they won't be poor any more. And we would be saints, which would just be quality. If you're a saint you can walk through fire, or do a miracle, or grow a big bushy beard like St Wilgefortis.'

'What's so good about growing a beard?'

'Wilgefortis was a woman. She grew it to avoid unwelcome male attention.' The unwelcome attention, by the way, was from the King of Sicily. Wilgefortis's dad wanted her to marry him. When she woke up with the beard, the King of Sicily changed his mind, which was exactly what she prayed for. Her father did have her crucified though. 'Come on, Anthony. It's a brilliant idea.'

He shook his head. 'Nice but not practical. Where would you find 458 poor people?'

'The world is full of poor people. The whole world is poor nearly. You've only got to look at the telly.'

'Yes, on the telly but not round here. There's no poor people round here. The house prices keep them out.' He explained about house pricing and social zoning. 'We live in an exclusive development, which means there are no poor people here. The only people who can afford to live here are nice people. You must've noticed. It's not like where we used to live.'

He was right. In St Francis's day, there were

lepers, beggars, mendicants, orphans and young women forced to sell their honour on every corner. Nowadays, you could walk from Cromarty Close to Great Ditton Primary every day for the rest of your life and never meet a young woman forced to sell her honour.

'Now, I've got an idea that *is* practical.'

'Go on.'

'We buy a house.'

'But we can't just spend it. It's been given to us for a higher purpose.'

'That's the beauty of it. When you buy a house, you're not spending the money. You're keeping it. It's called investing. Houses are always going up in price. If you buy a house now, for say 150,000 pounds, in ten years' time it will be worth maybe 300,000 pounds. So when you sell it, you will make 150,000 pounds' profit. That's called equity. You must have heard of equity.'

'I don't want equity.'

'It'll be great. We can get rid of all the money in one go, and when we're older sell the house, and we'll have even more money then than we've got now. And in the meantime, we can keep our stuff in there. It'd be better than your cardboard den.'

I tried to explain the difference between a den and a hermitage, but it fell on deaf ears.

In the estate agent's, Anthony went up to the counter, like it was a sweet shop, and said, 'Have you got any houses in Swindon?' He was mad on Swindon, because that's the place where house prices were going up fastest.

'Well, no,' said the woman. 'We only really do local. Most of our customers want a house where they actually live.'

'This is for an investment portfolio.'

'Oh, is it really? Oh, well, then. Is this a project for school?'

Anthony immediately invented a non-existent project, a non-existent school and a non-existent teacher. Honestly, if he was telling you this story, you wouldn't know which bits were true and which weren't.

The woman was very kind. She told him all about how mortgages work and she gave him piles of leaflets, describing available properties, mostly three-bedroom detached new-builds.

'What if you don't want a mortgage? What if you wanted to just pay all at once in cash?'

'Well, you'd need a wheelbarrow and a lot of security.'

Anthony laughed. He had to explain the funny side of this to me later. It was about how hard it would be to carry such a lot of cash. 'People don't really understand just how little 229,000 pounds really is,' he said sadly.

The minute we got home he went through all the leaflets, looking for a property that was not too near our house (in case Dad got suspicious) but not too far away (so we could keep an eye on it).

I did say, 'Anthony, this isn't right. We don't want a house. We've got a house. What's the point of having two houses? Think about it.'

He handed me one of the leaflets. It was a picture of our old house. Underneath, it said it was a character property with surviving period details, inc. fire surround, in a settled residential area. Two bedrooms, two reception, kitchen and separate utility room. And that was it. Nothing about us or what happened there. You wouldn't know it was our house except for the address.

I said, 'Why hasn't anyone bought it?'

'No one wants it. I told Dad to rent it out to

students. It doesn't matter. The insurance paid the mortgage off.'

'What insurance?'

'Never mind. Look at this. Number 17 Badger's Rake, conveniently placed for the Shopping City.'

If 229,000 pounds equals possibly 458 steps up the ladder, then spending 229,000 pounds on a house equals 458 steps down the ladder obviously. There is no patron saint of estate agents because no estate agent has ever become a saint. There have been saints who were sailors, blacksmiths, soldiers, bakers, teachers, housewives, swineherds, kings even. But in the whole of history, not one estate agent ever became a saint or even a blessed. It makes you think.

I have heard of people having a sinking feeling before, but I thought they were being metaphorical. When the taxi came to school and I discovered that Anthony had pre-booked it to take us to 17 Badger's Rake, I felt my stomach lurch, just the way it does in a lift. We went down and down and down, along the streets of the Old Town. The houses in Badger's Rake were even less saintly than ours. They had bay windows with criss-cross metal on them, fir trees all around and rapid, unimpeded access to the motor-way. At number 17, the lady from the estate agent's was already waiting on the doorstep.

Anthony jumped out of the car and shook her hand. 'We haven't got the money on us. But we can get it to you if you come to ours.'

'Oh, really,' said the woman. She didn't look as friendly as she did in the shop. 'Look, I've helped you with your project already. This is going a bit far. This is cheeky. I'm going to call your school and speak to the head teacher.'

'No. This isn't for the project. This is for our – my dad's – property portfolio. We – my dad – really wants to buy the house.'

'Well, then, where is he?'

'He said to start without him.'

'Start without him? How can we start without him? How can you show someone round a house who isn't here?'

Anthony pulled out the digital camera shaped like a pen. 'He gave us this. He said to take some pictures and show him later.'

The woman looked at her watch and opened the door. 'I need a pee anyway. You might as well come in.'

Anthony asked her if she thought the house would hold its value.

'I'm *on the toilet*, if you *don't* mind,' she shouted through the toilet door.

We went to look at the sunken bath in the en suite while we were waiting for her to come out. We heard a flush and then a shout.

'Come on. Out, the pair of you. Come on.' She was holding the front door open, for us to go out.

'We can offer 210,000, cash. And obviously there's no chain,' said Anthony. 'What do you think? Deal?'

He'd already explained to me that people would do anything for cash. So I was expecting her to say, 'Oh, thanks very much. It's all yours.' But she didn't. She glared at him and said, 'You are one cheeky little so-and-so,' then drove off in her Nissan Micra.

Divine intervention the only explanation.

It was a long walk back to the Shopping City and we didn't pass any buses, or any taxis. In fact, there wasn't even a pavement to speak of and it was getting dark. But I was so happy, the oncoming headlights seemed to be haloes dancing round us. One of the parakeets flew by. It flashed through the streetlight like a tongue of fire. I wanted to say something comforting to Anthony, but all I could think of was, 'I'm starving. Can we buy a pizza?'

'We can buy a Pizza *Hut* if we want to.'

'Just a pizza for now.'

And then – just outside Dixons – another miracle – a girl in a parka stepped in front of us and said, '*Big Issue*. Help the homeless.'

I gave her a tenner and told her to keep the change.

'Thanks, mate. I've had nothing to eat all day.'

'Oh. We're just going for a pizza. Come with us.'

'Brilliant.' The girl picked up her bag of magazines. She was going to come with us.

Anthony tried to put her off. 'She doesn't really want a pizza. She wants more money. We haven't got any more money.'

'No, I really fancy a pizza actually. Can I ask my friend?'

She nodded to a boy with a dog who was crouched in the doorway. 'Course you can,' I said. 'The more the merrier.'

The girl had five friends between Dixons and Pizza Hut. The waiter had to put two tables together to fit us all in. Two people had to share menus because there weren't enough to go round. They do a pizza that goes right to the edge of the pan, so it's an inch bigger in diameter than the normal one. It's called 'The Edge'. I had a Hawaiian Edge and so did the girl in the parka. Two of her mates had a Farmhouse Edge. One of them had spicy beef. Anthony and the other two had Meat Feasts. Everyone had garlic bread with extra garlic. And we all went to the salad bar. It was amazing. It was the most food I've seen in one place since First Communion. Six meals equals six good deeds equals six rungs surely.

I said, 'This is fantastic. Anthony said there were no poor people round here because of house prices, but there's loads of you.'

They all wanted pudding. Anthony was against this, but then it turned out that they had an Ice Cream Factory – it's a yellow machine that lets you serve yourself ice cream and then you can put chocolate shavings or hundreds and thousands or tiny marshmallows on top, and three different sauces. It was completely quality. I wondered if pudding constituted a separate good deed from the actual pizza. In which case we were looking at twelve rungs.

*

'You see,' I said as we got on the bus. 'We helped the poor and we had those little marshmallow things. That is what we should be doing every day.'

The bill came to 175 quid. Anthony took out his calculator and worked out how many times we'd have to do that to get rid of all the money. 'That's 1,303.517. Call that tips. Which mean 1,300 trips to Pizza Hut. And d'you know how many days we've got to get rid of this money?'

The answer was twelve.

If you've got an idea, twelve days is plenty of time. I had a brilliant idea and it would have worked too, if it hadn't been for people.

The Latter-day Saints people all dressed the same in white shirts and black jackets, and all carried the same smart black briefcases. They always left the house together, walking in a line, and as they passed you they would each nod at you, one after the other, like ducks in a shooting gallery. Anthony thought they were too conspicuous.

'Look at them,' he'd say. 'Like penguins in a playground. And you know where they're going with the briefcases, don't you?'

'Of course! To help the poor?' I don't know

why I hadn't thought of it before. They called themselves saints. There must be a reason for it. 'They go and help the poor.'

'The launderette. Look.'

It was true. If you looked carefully, there was always a corner of undie sticking out of the smart black briefcase. So they had no washing machine and they had no cars. They all lived together in the same house and in the daytime they all went off together like the twelve Apostles. You know what they were? They were a set of rungs waiting to be climbed. That was my brilliant idea: give the money to the Latter-day Saints.

After school the next day, I sat on their wall and waited till the first one came home. 'Excuse me,' I said. 'Do you help the poor?'

'What poor? Excuse me?' He had a strong accent, like a footballer. Maybe he was from Sweden or Holland.

'Any.'

'You're asking for money?'

'No.'

'We have no cash kept on the premises. Don't take the wrong idea from our respectable clothing. We live simply. No dishwasher. No cable TV.

No microwave, even though I don't see why not personally. Also, no car obviously.'

'So you're poor?'

'In a sense, yes.'

I managed to shove 7,000 pounds through their letter box that night when I was supposed to be taking the rubbish out. After the first few hundred, I got worried that it seemed to be taking ages, so I prayed for help and St Nicholas turned up. He explained that it was easier to drop it down the chimney. I explained to him about solar heating. After we'd done about 4,000, St Nicholas got bored and cross. It was his busiest time of year. He said, '*Noli sollicitum esse. Pauperes semper nobiscum erunt.*' (*Don't worry about it. The poor will always be with us.*) And we walked back to the house.

I asked him if he'd ever come across a St Maureen.

'*Quis?*'

'Maureen.'

'*Dubito, etsi raro in publicum prodeo.*' (*I don't think so, but then I don't get out much.*)

'Except at this time of year obviously.'

'*Sane.*'

If we're saying 500 pounds equals one rung,

then 4,000 is eight rungs. Plus I helped Santa on his round! Quality!

I was on a roll. I wasn't even surprised when I spotted another rung in the playground, before school had started. When the second whistle went, we all walked quickly to our lines and I was in front of Barry.

He leaned into my ear and said, 'Pringles.'

I passed them back to him.

The girl with the lovely corn rows was in the next line. She said, 'Why don't you buy your own Pringles?'

'Don't need to. I eat everyone else's.' Barry popped the lid of mine and winked at me.

It was the wink that put the thought in my head. I thought, Hello, is this another rung? And I said, 'Barry, are you poor?'

Barry's left eyelid had still not come up from its wink. Now it fluttered a bit, then it opened wide, wide, wide and stared into mine.

'What?'

'Are you poor?'

He hit me very hard across the face. I remembered to turn the other cheek. He hit me in the stomach. I had to sit on the floor to get my breath back. He put his shoe next to my face and said, 'See that shoe? What does it say on it?'

It said, Rockport.

'Would I have Rockports if I was poor?' And then he kicked me and I couldn't breathe for what seemed like a long weekend.

Now this might sound like it wasn't that successful, but that depends how you look at it. It's true I didn't help a poor person but I did try, so that's got to be worth a rung, and, more importantly, I did suffer persecution, which is just fantastic. I mean, five rungs at least. In fact, as I was lying on the tarmac, I actually did start to feel a bit floaty, like I might rise up into Heaven. Anthony said that this was due to a change in air pressure inside my head caused by the loss of blood from my nose.

It was the blood that made the girl with the lovely corn rows start screaming. Mr Quinn came running over. Barry kept saying, 'D'you know what he said? D'you know what he said?'

Mr Quinn sent him to the head and told the girl with the corn rows to take me off to the quiet corner while I recovered my equilibrium. She got me a drink of water and sat chatting to me. She told me her name was Gemma and asked me lots of questions, such as, 'What team does your Anthony support?' and 'What music does your Anthony like?' and 'Does your Anthony ever go to the Early Bird session at the baths first thing on a Saturday, because it's free if you've got your leisure pass? Tell him.'

On the way home, I asked Anthony, 'What's so special about Rockports?'

'Rockports! That's a great idea. We could both have a pair.'

'But why?'

'They're great. You tuck the laces in the side instead of tying them. Dead, you know, state-of-the-art.'

'And they really hurt if someone kicks you with them.'

'Right. We'll get some.'

Surprisingly, there actually was a St Gemma. Her name was Gemma Galgani (1878–1903). She was an ecstatic who excelled in the practice of heroic poverty and her feast is 11 April. I was in the hermitage, trying to look up heroic poverty, when someone said, 'Anyone there?'

I looked out. There was a man in a Tommy Hilfiger jacket with lots of stubble on his face. The stubble made me think it might be St Damian of Molokai, who was a bit rough, though very good. But that didn't really tie in with the Hilfiger jacket. He definitely wasn't Gemma Galgani. I said, 'I don't know who you are.'

He said, 'Mutual that, then.'

I tried to look him in the eye, but I realized that one eye was looking straight at me and the other was looking off to the left. I wasn't sure which eye to look into.

'This yours?' he asked, pointing at the hermitage.

I nodded.

'Very nice. Close to the railway. What's inside?'

He bent down and peeped in. He couldn't see the scooters or the Airzooka because they were still covered by the tartan blanket. He put his hand in and rooted around. He found the little tube. 'What's this?'

'Tinted moisturizer.'

He nodded and looked off into the distance. He threw the tube to me.

'What are you looking for?'

'Money. Know anything about that?'

This was brilliant. This was the second opportunity in one day.

I said, 'Are you poor?'

'What?'

The minute I said it there was a crackling sound and then a crackling voice saying, 'Damian, Damian . . .' Even I jumped a bit, but the stubbly man sort of bounced with shock.

'What the hell is that?'

I showed him the walkie-talkie wristwatch. 'It's my brother. My turn to set the table. You wait here.'

'Now, you hang on . . .'

'No, honest. I'll be back with it.'

'With what?'

'The money. I've got tons of it.'

I ran off.

Anthony was standing in the garden because the walkie-talkie wristwatch didn't work through walls. Well, it did, but it picked up Red Rose Radio. He was leaning over the fence, looking towards the railway. You could still see the man, standing up on the railway embankment.

'Who's that, then?'

'Poor person. Yet another poor person. And you said there weren't any.'

'What's he waiting for?'

'I'm going to give him some money.'

I was going into the house. Anthony pulled me back. 'What've you said?'

'I've told him we've got loads of money.'

'Oh, Damian.'

'What?'

'Nothing. Nothing. Leave it to me.'

Anthony went and got the big bottle we'd been saving the change in. It weighed a ton. 'We'll give him this.'

'Can't we give him a few hundred quid as well? Like 500.'

'No, we can't.'

'Why not?'

'I'll tell you why not later. Come on.'

We went back up to the railway. He was wait- ing for us. When Anthony held out the big bottle, he just stared at it. Or possibly he was staring at me.

'See?' said Anthony. 'Loads of money. We've been saving it for ages. For the poor. We try to be good. Take it.'

The man didn't move. Anthony put the bottle down on the grass. 'We've got to go now. Teatime.'

The man didn't say anything, didn't touch the bottle. He watched us when we were walking back across the field.

'I don't think we gave him enough money.'

'We gave him plenty. Go round the front way,' said Anthony. 'I don't want him to know which is our house.'

'Why not?'

'Because it's dangerous. You've got to be careful. Some people in the world are greedy, Damian. Money makes them act weird. You've got to be careful. Have you told anyone else about it?'

'Not really. Not told.'

'What have you done?'

'I've tried to be good.'

'Damian . . .'

But he stopped talking then. We were just coming into Cromarty Close from the top end and a taxi had passed us and pulled up. The Latter-day Saints started to pile out. The Latter-day Saints and their recent purchases. One was carrying a microwave. Another had a blender. And another had a foot spa. Anthony was so cross, he had to sit down on the wall.

It was a pity he did that really. If he'd just gone inside he wouldn't have seen the Comet van pull up and unload the DVD player, the dishwasher, the Gamecube and the *two* plasma-screen televisions. It wasn't the fact that I'd given them the money that upset him. It was the fact that they'd managed to spend it.

'Look at all the stuff that they've got! And what have we got? Junk. Junk that people were going to give to Oxfam anyway. Two tellies, a dishwasher . . .'

He went on and listed everything they'd bought. He did this ten times, like a rosary. It was a very impressive feat of memory.

'I didn't know they were going to buy a telly. I thought they were going to give it away. They're supposed to be saints, after all. I thought they were going to give it to the poor. I thought they *were* poor.'

'Look, Damian, if you give poor people money, what happens to them? They stop being poor. Obviously. And if they're not poor any more, what are they? They're the same as everyone else.'

So that was when I had this worrying thought: what if giving people more money just makes people more money-ish? And if it does, what's all the money for? What can we do with it?

After supper, there was a knock on the door. Dad answered it and it was one of the Latter-day Saints – Eli – carrying a little box and looking very anxious. Anthony and I were washing up. We looked at each other nervously.

'Probably going to ask for more money,' growled Anthony.

Eli said he had an idea he wished to share with us. Then he opened his box and took out a tiny camera. 'This is a security camera, CCTV. It mounts easily to the door lintel using the bracket arrangement here and then hooks up very simply to your domestic television.'

Anthony sniffed bitterly and said, 'Television? Or televisions?'

Eli didn't notice.

'We're most anxious about this very high likelihood of a burglary in the area. Terry says he has seen a suspicious character and of course we must protect our property. This camera could be most useful in this regard. We have bought three such. We wish to position one with a clear line of vision across the main point of access to the Close – from your front door to the car port of number 3. The ideal positioning would be your lintel. Would you be willing to assist the community in this way?'

I said, 'I thought you didn't mind about burglaries. I thought you didn't care about earthly goods.'

'Well, of course in a sense this is true, but if

we do not have security, then we are tempting the burglar, not so? And so tempting him into sin. We therefore become assistants to the sin. The camera comes with reactive halogen lighting, which has a prohibitive effect.'

'Great,' said Dad.

Personally, I went to bed.

I lay there listening to Dad clanging up and down the stepladder and drilling holes for the CCTV bracket, then I fell asleep. It felt like I'd been asleep for hours when I heard him calling us. Anthony and I hurried downstairs to see what was up. He was very excited. 'Just sit there,' he said, pointing to the couch.

We sat down. He turned the TV on and started flicking through the channels. 'One, two, three, four, five and now . . .' Six was a picture of the car port of number 3, which had a life-size illuminated Santa sitting outside. 'That's the terrestrial channels and the new CCTV. That much we know. Now . . . seven, eight, nine, ten . . .' He went through all the new channels, with a big happy grin on his face.

Anthony smiled too and said, 'Brilliant, Dad. How did you do it?'

'I was just fixing the CCTV and there it was. It must be something to do with the cable. Maybe it acts as a kind of aerial. Maybe it's a miracle.' It was the first time we'd seen him smile in ages. 'Thank you, God.'

I explained that St Clare was the patron saint of television. 'If it is a miracle, it's one of hers.'

'Right. Well, what d'you fancy watching?'

We all watched the repeat of *Monster Truck Tug of War* until we realized Dad had fallen asleep. We didn't know what to do with him. We couldn't carry him upstairs. We took off his shoes, moved his feet up on to the couch and covered him with the small duvet. We weren't sure whether to turn the telly off or not.

I said, 'Couldn't we tell him about the money? Just to cheer him up?'

Anthony said, 'If you want to cheer him up, tell him a joke.'

Outside, the reactive halogen lamp kept going on and off. It didn't have any prohibitive effect on cats.

11

Just to be logical about things: if it's wrong to give money to people, then it must be right to take it off people. If it's right to take it off people, then burglars and bank robbers are good people, which they're not. Therefore, it's *not* wrong to give money away. You just have to find the right people to give it to.

And I had to find them in the next ten days.

Every week during Art, Mr Quinn writes a title on the board and you can do a drawing, make a collage, build a model, whatever. This week he wrote 'If I Got a Million Euros for Christmas . . .'

Thank you, Mr Quinn.

Everyone ran for the bendy-straws box – bendy-straw sculptures were the big thing that term – and got going on bendy-straw yachts, houses, cars, everything. Personally, I was staring at a big blank sheet of paper. I stared at it so long that I thought I was going to fall into it and be swallowed up in icy-white nothing.

'I'll do you a drawing if you're stuck.' It was Tricia Springer, who was the best at art.

'Would you, honest?'

'Sure. Could do you a yacht, or a car, or a house. That's what most people have gone for. Or we could think outside the box – maybe a rocket, or horses, or a nice stretch of land.'

'I just can't think. What would you like to draw?'

'I can draw horses out of my own head. Fifty quid each.'

'How d'you mean?'

'I'll draw you one horse for fifty quid, two for 100, a herd for, you know, maybe 300. We could do a discount for anything over six. Obviously I won't have to draw all their feet because some of them will be partly obscured.'

'Why's it so expensive?'

'It's not. You gave some kid a tenner for fetching your hot lunch for you the other day. This is my talent you're buying here. I am the best at art.'

'When I came to school on your bike, you said you didn't need ten pounds.'

'Times have changed. Where would a tenner get you in this school now? It's a tenner for ten minutes on Keegan's Gamecube. And it's all down to you.'

I gave her 100 quid for two horses without saddles but with some mountains in the background.

I tried to discuss things with Anthony at Small Play. 'It's terrible. Everyone's got money but no one's any richer because everyone just charges more. I mean, 100 quid for a picture and it was felt pen. She wanted more for paints.'

'Is she any good?'

'That's not the point.'

'It is for me. Term's over soon. Dad's going to want to see my model of Tracy Island, the one I won the Subbuteo for.'

'She's the best at art.'

'Which one is she?'

I pointed her out. He ended up paying her another 100 for the model and she wanted fifty up front, even though the model wouldn't be ready till the last week of term.

'It'll be worth it,' said Anthony. 'What d'you think of the Rockports?'

He showed me his new shoes. They were red, with the laces tucked in at the side.

I said, 'Won't Dad notice that you've got new shoes?'

'He never notices anything. But I'm not sure about them anyway. Now that everyone's got money, everyone's got Rockports. They're losing their prestige value.'

'I need to ponder things in my heart,' I said.

I walked back across the playground with my eyes downcast, which is how I noticed that I was now the only boy not wearing Rockports.

After school, I decided to go home via the hermitage. I ducked through the holly and stopped still. The hermitage was flat. I don't mean the wind had blown it over or the rain had battered it. I mean someone had taken off every bit of masking tape, piece by piece, and folded the cardboard boxes flat. They'd even folded the tartan travel rug. The micro-scooters were out of their boxes and the boxes were squashed flat and neatly packed on top of the others. It was all really neat, except for my statue of St Francis, which was in hundreds of sharp little pieces, thrown all over the mud.

I was already frightened when I heard someone behind me. I spun around to face a tall man in a bright blue robe.

'St Charles Lwanga (d. 1885), martyr of Uganda,' I said.

'That's right.' He held out his hand for me to shake. It was covered in blood. 'Sorry about that. I was beheaded, you know.'

'I know. Did you do this?'

'No. But we can help you put it right. There's enough of us.'

It was only when he said this that I noticed all the other martyrs of Uganda were also there. Twenty-two of them in fantastic costumes, all waving at me.

'Beheading was very big in Uganda at the time. Some of us were in construction before we got into martyrdom. We'll do what we can, but I can't promise anything. You've had some right cowboys in here.'

'Do you know who did it?'

He looked off into the distance. 'I can lend a

hand but I can't point the finger. You'll have to figure it out yourself.'

And they all set to work fixing the hermitage, and singing the most beautiful song I'd ever heard. It rose and fell like waves on the sea and sometimes one voice would call out above all the others, like a bird appearing in the sunset. While they were singing, two African greys appeared and sat on the railway fence, as though they were listening.

'I enjoy those birds. They make me feel at home. Did you set them free?'

'Yes. Like St Francis, you know. What's the song about?'

'It's about water. In Uganda now, people have to pay for water. Sometimes as much as 10 per cent of their income. That's privatization for you. Don't talk to me about the I M F and the World Bank.'

'OK, I won't, then.'

'People can't afford to wash their own hands, so they get diseases. You don't need fancy hospitals and drugs to keep people feeling better. You just need cheap fresh water. Did you know that you can dig a well for as little as 1,000 pounds?'

'No, I didn't know that. That is the most enjoyable news ever! Is it true?'

'Completely true.'

Anthony seemed almost as excited as I was when I told him. He was on givemeoneofthose.com, staring at the screen while a picture of the scuba scooter (£325.00 plus P and P) was downloading. He said, 'That is fantastic. A thousand pounds for a well. You could buy two.'

'I was thinking of buying 220.'

He bit his lip. 'Oh. Right.'

'Yes. There's a charity. They build wells. We give them the money. They build the wells. We are sorted.'

'And how're you going to give them the money? Pop 220 grand in the post? Have you felt the weight of it? Let me show you something. See this website? You can buy quad bikes. You can buy scuba scooters – that's underwater motorbikes. We can afford them. We can afford a fleet of them. Can we buy them? NO. Because you need a credit card. Or you need to go to the shop, and we can't because we're kids. What's your charity called?'

It was called Water Aid. We Googled around till we found it. It was based in Shrewsbury.

'Now, you tell me how you're going to get to Shrewsbury with a bag full of money.'

I said, 'They'll collect. Oxfam collected when we gave them that wardrobe from the old house. I'm sure the water people'll just come and collect the cash.'

Anthony stared at me. He knew I was right. He went back to his Googling.

I said, 'I'll just call them now, then, shall I?'

'If you like. If you're sure that's what you want to do with the money.'

'Oh, definitely. D'you know how much difference a well can make to an African village? I'll tell you . . .'

'I'm sure it's great. And after all, India's not your problem, is it?'

'How d'you mean?'

'Well, they need wells in India too. And Afghanistan. They're desperate in Afghanistan, but, like I said, if you prefer Africa . . .'

He'd brought up a picture of a little girl with dust in her hair, standing in a pile of rubble somewhere in Iraq. Then another picture of a boy with one leg in Kosovo. Then another of a baby with a huge belly in Mozambique.

'As you said, Damian, why should you care?'

'I did not say that. Maybe we could divide the money . . . maybe we could—'

'Did you know this, by the way? That you can prevent river blindness with an injection that costs less than a pound? Quarter of a million quid, you could more or less wipe out river blindness.'

'Well, that would be good, but . . .'

'But what?'

'I don't know what to do now.'

'Think it over.'

I sat on the end of the bed, staring at the carpet. I stared at it so long it started to feel as if the bed was moving.

'I didn't mean you to think it over right now. Maybe you should sleep on it.'

I looked up. Anthony was staring at a picture of a woman on his monitor. He'd been Googling again.

'What're you doing?'

'See these women? You can buy them. Look, this one's called Victoria. Price – £39.99.'

'Let's have a look. Are you sure?'

He pushed me away. 'Spam for brains. It's an underwear website. Look.' He zoomed in on a lacy bra. A swirl of black and pink pixels swished across the screen. 'See that? You can see it protruding. That's her nipple.'

It looked like more pixels to me. 'What's it for?'

'Well, it's for feeding babies.'

'Did Mum have one, then?'

'She had two. They've all got two.'

'Did she feed us with them, then?'

'Yeah. I remember.'

'You do not remember being a baby.'

'I remember you, though. I remember her feeding you.'

I looked at Victoria for a while. Even after Anthony had logged off, I could still see her in my brain while I was lying in bed. I imagined that you could really send off for her for £39.99 and that she'd come and we'd drive down to Shrewsbury together and be excellent and go whoosh to the top of the ladder.

12

To be physical about it, water is amazing. Human beings are over 80 per cent water. And the surface of the earth is nearly 70 per cent water. From outer space, it looks like a drop of water. To be economical about it, most things that are precious, like gold or jewels, are precious because they're in short supply. There's more water than there is almost anything else, but it's still more precious than gold. So precious that some people in dry areas are prepared to spend most of the day just fetching and carrying it. In some countries, the women set out at three or four o'clock every morning to collect water, so that they can be back in time to begin the day. No one would do that for gold. And gold or jewels are still valuable if they're not quite right. It's not the same with water. To be chemical about it, if water's got the wrong amount of salt in it, or toxins, you can die of thirst next to an ocean full of it. If you can give people enough water, you can change their lives. If those women didn't have to leave their villages so early in the morning, imagine how much more time they'd have to spend with their children, or just being asleep. If you can get even a little bit of water on to a farm, you can grow maize and keep chickens and have just enough to eat. But if you can get a lot of water on to that same farm, you could grow peas, bananas, pineapples, mangoes, sweet potatoes, eucalyptus trees – you name it – and make money and send your children to school and never be poor again.

I could see it in my mind, a trail of water running across the desert, and all around it green shoots shooting and leaves spreading, and grass waving and fruit getting fatter and fatter, and the whole desert coming to life like a page in a colouring book. Then I woke up and found I'd wet myself.

I haven't done that since Mum was in the best place. Luckily Dad had already gone to work and Anthony was still asleep. I stripped the bed and washed the sheets on the 40° setting (colour-fast cottons), along with some towels and my pyjamas. I tried to think of it all as mortification, but by the time I pressed the 'start' button, I felt like going back to bed. But I couldn't because there was no bedding and anyway it was a school day. I'm really glad I didn't too, because that was the day I first saw Dorothy.

I think I might've seen her before anyone else did. I was hanging up my coat and she went by, chatting to Mr Quinn. She had her hair in corn rows like Gemma and she wore a smart jacket, like the ladies on the make-up counter. She was carrying a little flip-top bin.

When the whistle went, we were all told to go to the hall instead of our classrooms as someone was coming to give us a special assembly.

'In classes and in silence please,' said Mr James, the head teacher. He was wearing his reindeer tie.

We were shuffling into our lines, when suddenly there was a scream from the Year Five row. Everyone was standing on their toes and pushing forward, trying to see what was going on.

Mr James said, 'Everybody . . . everybody . . . just take a step back and then everyone can see.' He winked at the smart lady, who was on the stage with him now.

Everyone made a big circle and there in the middle of the circle was Shumita and the little flip-top bin I'd seen earlier. It didn't seem that interesting. Until the flip-top flipped open and a voice came out. It said, '*So what's your name?*'

'Oh, my God,' said Shumita.

'*Hello, Oh-My-God,*' said the bin, and everyone laughed.

'Shumita. My name's Shumita.'

'*I like your pigtails, Shumita,*' said the bin.

'Oh, that is bad. It can see me. How can it see me?'

'*Don't be alarmed. I come in peace.*' It had a nice soft voice.

One of the Year Sixes barged past her to get a better look.

The bin said, '*No pushing please. No pushing.*'

'I'm enjoying this,' said the Year Six.

'*What's your name?*' said the bin.

'How's it doing it?'

'*How do you do, How's-It-Doing-It?*'

I looked back towards the stage. Mr James was grinning all over his face. The smart lady seemed to be talking quietly to herself. She had her finger in her ear and she was holding something that looked like a pen quite close to her mouth.

I don't want to be cynical about it, but I knew it was her working the bin, that it was her voice we were listening to. She tucked the pen-shaped thing into her pocket and asked Shumita to bring her the bin.

Everyone went quiet, expecting her to explain it.

Instead she shouted, 'Who cares about poor people?'

I couldn't believe it.

My hand shot up. So did everyone else's, which means that not everyone is completely honest. She started to tell us about the euro and the changeover. She wanted to know how much a pound was worth in euros. Everyone knew. Then she wanted to know how much two pee was worth. No one's hand went up for a while.

She said, 'I'll tell you. It's worth . . . not very much. But how many people are here? Let's count, shall we?'

She started pointing at people and counting them off. When she got to thirteen, she said, 'I'm sure I've counted you twice,' and Mr James said, 'It's 368. At this assembly. There's 368.'

'Thank you, sir. So what is 368 times two?'

I put my hand up because I wanted to be the one to tell her. She pointed at me and I realized that I didn't actually know the answer. It was our Anthony who said, 'It's 736.'

'That's right. Seven pounds and thirty-six pee, which in euros is . . . ten euros and thirty-seven cents. Now that's still not very much here, but in Ethiopia, that will buy you a bag of seed corn that could see a family through the autumn. Imagine that. That's for just two pee each. Now what would happen if you gave me four pee each? How much would I have?'

I put my had up again and said, 'Twenty euros and seventy-four cents.'

'Perfect. Here. This is for you.'

She held out a yellow plastic currency converter shaped like the Euro Duck. I had to walk up to the stage to collect it from her. She carried on talking, but ruffled my hair as I walked back to my place.

'But what if you gave me seven euros fifty from now till the end of term? What could we do then? I bet we could build a well.'

I shouted, 'Yes!'

She looked across at me and smiled. 'Well,

someone thinks that's a good idea,' she said. 'And I'm not surprised.' She rubbed my hair again as she strolled past me and started telling everyone all sorts of things about wells, which I already knew. I just kept nodding all the time she was talking. She said, 'When we change over, you won't get much for your small change. But it could mean a lot to other people. It's no good to you so . . . CHUCK IT IN THE BIN!!!'

People started piling five pees and two pees into the bin just to hear it say, '*Thank you*' or '*Is that all? Come on, you must have a bit more.*'

As I passed it, the bin went, '*What about you, then? What's your name?*'

I said, 'Damian.'

'*Got any money for me, Damian?*'

I nodded and looked up at her. She was looking right at me. Trying to not let anyone see, I put all the money that was in my pocket into the bin, then looked up at her. She winked at me and the bin moved off.

Anthony came up behind me and whispered, 'What did you just do?'

'Same as everyone else. Put money in the bin.'

'How much money?'

'Just what I had on me.'

'Which was?'

'A couple of grand. Maybe three.'

'Three grand! What did you bring three grand to school for?'

'In case. You know. You wouldn't understand.'

'Can't you see that's suspicious?'

'It's not suspicious. It's unusual, but it's not suspicious. How can it be suspicious? It's our money.'

Anthony looked at me long and hard. 'OK,' he said, 'it's time you knew the truth.'

When we got home, Anthony showed me a site he'd bookmarked. It's one of his favourites. It gives all the world news, but with a financial slant. So if it was covering the Olympics, it'd tell you how much the gold medals were worth. In the archive section, there was a picture of a train. Underneath it said, 'Tons of Money'.

'Click on it,' said Anthony.

'What for?'

'You'll see what for.'

This is what came up:

Sadly for most of us, the phrase 'tons of money' is just a figure of speech. But yesterday thieves made off with literally 'tons of money', in used, high-denomination sterling notes, earmarked for destruction in the government incinerator near Warrington. The robbery was planned with military precision and a relatively low capital outlay. The final haul could be something in the region of £6,000,000.

LINKS: Brilliant robberies of history, click here.
What would you do with 'tons of money'?
Message board, click here.

I said, 'What's this got to do with us?' 'Read on.'

HOW TO LOSE £6,000,000.
COUNTDOWN TO THAT SUPER-RAID
Last updated 1 December, 7.00 a.m.

From 16:00 'Trackfinder' personnel and Transport Police secure Platform 1, King's Cross, and begin loading twelve and a half tons of paper sterling on to a freight train. The money is marked for incineration as part of the 'Big Switch Over' to the euro on 17 December.

18:55 Train is fully laden and ready to depart. Operators are told there will be no Railtrack 'departure slot' until 20:00 (Railtrack charge for clearing King's Cross–Warrington route: €70,000).

19:05 A van bearing the official Railtrack livery appears at one end of the platform. The van was a three-year-old Ford Rascal (RRP €9,000).

CLICK HERE FOR WWW.FORD.CO.UK
FOR THE BEST DEALS ON VANS AND SALOONS

19:07 Van drives at full speed towards security guards. Guards scatter and ten men in replica Newcastle United shirts (RRP €49.99) and balaclavas leap out and begin laying about them with baseball bats, gaining access to the body of the train.

CLICK HERE FOR TOONARMYSHOP.COM – PREMIER
SUPPLIERS OF NEWCASTLE UNITED OFFICIAL
MERCHANDISING, REPLICA KITS AND PROGRAMMES

CLICK HERE FOR 'QUICKTIME' MOVIE FILE – CCTV
FOOTAGE OF VIOLENT INCIDENT (REQUIRES QUICKTIME
5 OR LATER)

By 19:12 Transport police, dog handlers and an armed rapid-reaction unit were on the scene. The robbers return to van and drive off at speed and with a reckless disregard for life. They had been on the train for only ninety seconds. Security ascertains that only one sealed packet of notes was missing.

122

LINK: To view TV footage of Police Statement (requires Quicktime 5 or later), click here.

From 19:16 The van is pursued by the police. It is quickly abandoned in a city side street, the robbers making their get-away on foot. The police give chase as far as Norfolk Road, but here it becomes clear why the robbers had chosen this day and this location. Last night was the Arsenal versus Newcastle United premiership clash (attendance 39,000 at an average spend of €40.00). The street is thronged with Newcastle fans, many thousands wearing replica shirts identical to those worn by the robbers, who simply melt into the crowd.

19:40 Transport police return to abandoned vehicle to discover that the missing packet of money (£50,000) is still in the back of the van. This is returned to King's Cross.

23:50 The train is finally cleared for departure. It looked as though the robbery had been foiled.

This was the bottom of the page. I said, 'OK. I've read it. So what?'

Then Anthony scrolled down a bit further for me.

1 December The train arrives at the depot and the real nature of the robbery is discovered. The violent incident at the station was not a robbery at all but simply a distraction. Ten robbers had jumped on to the train but only nine had escaped in the van. One member of the gang remained hidden among the pallets of cash. As soon as the train moved off, he began his work of ripping open the packets and stuffing money into dozens of JJB sports holdalls (RRP €42.99). Whenever the train slowed down for a bend, he threw out a bag of cash. Each bag contained something in the region of £250,000. At each bend a member of the gang was waiting to retrieve the bag. Between King's Cross and Warrington something in the region of £6,000,000 was flung from the train. On the journey, the robber changed out of his Newcastle shirt and into an official 'Trackfinder' overall. On arrival he mingled with the porters and fork-lift operatives as they unloaded the train, taking the first opportunity to exit the station. The division of the money into relatively small amounts means it should be easy to change it into euros (current rate 71 pence to the euro) before the switchover. A bag left unrecovered near Nuneaton was found this morning, providing a vital clue in the reconstruction of the story. Other drops were very likely made near Crewe, Stafford, Penkridge and Watford, among other places.

LINKS: For a map of that journey, including slow bends, click here.

Your chance to find a bag of cash, click here.

Anthony had been reading it over my shoulder. He was smiling. 'You have to hand it to them,' he said.

'Hand what to them?'

'Well, it was brilliant, wasn't it? Six million. In unmarked notes. Completely undetectable. No one was even hurt. And the money was going to be burned anyway. So it wasn't even a robbery at all in one way. It was more like recycling.'

At first I couldn't think of anything to say. Then I said, 'Shut up!'

'What?'

'What did you have to go and do that for? Why couldn't you keep it to yourself?'

'Damian . . .'

'I saw it. It fell out of the sky.'

'You saw it fall off the back of a train.'

'Shut up! Shut up! Shut up! Why d'you have to tell me?'

'Because you need to know. Because the people who did this, they're dangerous. They dropped the money all over the country. So there must be dozens of them. If one of them was supposed to collect a bag and got there late, what would happen then? Someone else might have found it. Someone like you. D'you think they'd just say, oh dear, never mind? Or d'you think they'd go looking for it? They'd come looking for it, Damian, looking for you, and they could be anyone – a man with a glass eye, a woman with corn rows, some people with funny accents and unfeasibly white shirts. You've got to be careful. They'll want their money back and they'll want it quick. They've only got a few days left to change it.'

'I thought it came from God.'

'What?'

'Who else would have that much cash?'

'Well, maybe it did. After all, God does move in mysterious ways.'

'He does not rob banks. God does not rob banks. All right?'

Whenever things get theological, Anthony stops listening. He just said, 'Well, if he didn't, who did? Just think about that.'

On Monday morning, during Numeracy Hour, Mr James came into our class, which he never normally does. He made us put down our pencils and look at him. He looked very serious.

'Last week,' Mr James said, 'you may recall a lady came to the school on behalf of Change for Change. She's here with me now and she's got something she wants to ask you. I want you to listen politely and to answer her questions honestly.'

He opened the door and the smart lady came in. Mr James stood next to her while she was talking, staring at us one by one.

She said, 'On Friday I asked you to give up your change and you responded generously. Very generously. But one person gave a big donation. A worryingly big donation, to be honest. And we just need to know where that donation came from, so that we know it's . . . well . . . legal really. So if the person who made that donation could come forward, that would be great.'

I really was about to put my hand up and say, 'It was me,' when Tricia jumped out of her seat and said it was her.

Mr James looked at her. 'How much did you put in, Tricia, if you don't mind me asking?'

'I put ten pounds in.'

'Well,' said the smart lady, 'that was very kind, but . . .'

Mr James butted in. 'Where did you get ten pounds, Tricia?'

She turned her head towards me just a little bit as she said, 'I sold something, sir, and then when the lady told us about the water, I just wanted to do something. Sorry, sir . . .'

'Don't be silly. What you did was excellent. Really. Well done.'

She never mentioned that what she'd sold was a drawing of two horses with some mountains in the background *and no saddles* for 100 pounds.

'But that's not what we're looking for.' He looked around the class. 'I think the best thing would be for whoever did this to come to my office some time – any time – today. As I said, we just need to know where it came from.'

And he left.

All through Numeracy Hour, I thought about what I was going to say. By the time the bell went for Small Play, I had it all worked out. I went straight to Mr James's office, practising my speech. 'We didn't know it was stolen,' I was going to say. 'We want to give it to the poor. The government wants to burn it just because it's old, which is wicked. OK, it's a bit tatty, some of it, but nothing a bit of Sellotape wouldn't fix, and the poor people of this world don't care what money looks like . . .' I wasn't sure the bit about the Sellotape was entirely necessary. I was trying to decide when I realized that someone had got there before me. A surprising person. Our Anthony.

'What are you doing here?' I whispered.

'I knew you'd tell them. I wasn't going to let you do it on your own. I've got interests to protect here.'

Before I could argue back, Mr James opened the door, called us in and told us to sit down.

I'd never been in Mr James's office before. You have to be really bad to go in there. There's a clock on the wall with the numbers going round the wrong way. The hands go round the wrong way too. You'd think that if you looked at it long enough it'd give you the feeling that time could go backwards. It doesn't work like that, though. It makes you feel like time is coming at you from all directions.

'OK,' said Mr James. 'The Cunningham brothers, eh? What do you want to tell me?'

I said, 'I put the . . .'

Anthony said, 'We made the big donation. To Change for Change.'

'I did,' I said, 'it was me actually.'

'But it was both our money.'

'I'm sure it was. It's just . . . well, if you don't mind me asking, where exactly did you get the money?'

I started, 'Well, at first I thought it had just fallen from the . . .'

But before I got any further, Anthony said, 'Stole it.'

Mr James stared.

Anthony said, 'We stole it from some neighbours.'

Neighbours?

Mr James said, 'Don't say any more.' Then he held his hand up to stop us talking and phoned Dad. 'Mr Cunningham? I think you'd better come to the school if that's possible. We have a situation.'

It took seventeen backwards minutes for Dad to get to the school. Mr James explained that he didn't want to talk to us until Dad got there as that was the proper procedure. He did some phone calls and marked some books while we sat in silence. I wanted to shout at Anthony, but I didn't dare.

When Dad came in, his hair was all sticking up at the front. Whenever he's confused or worried, Dad pushes his fingers backwards through his hair and it stays sticking up. So he must have been doing a lot of that while he was driving over.

'After what we've been through,' said Dad, scowling at me, then at Anthony, then at me again, 'after all that, you lied to me. Because that's the worst part, not the thieving, the lying.'

Mr James coughed. 'Actually the thieving is quite bad. The stealing that is. The stealing is quite bad. If you did steal it. Did you steal it?'

He looked at me. And I realized I could tell the truth now and it would all make sense and they'd take charge of the money and everything would be all right. I said, 'No. We didn't. Well, we . . .'

Anthony said, 'We did steal it. We stole it from them people.'

'What people?'

'The people with the shirts, you know. In our road. The morons.'

'Mormons!' Dad went bright red. 'You stole money from Mormons?'

I said, 'No,' and Anthony said, 'Yes.' Somehow Anthony was more convincing. He almost convinced me.

Dad pushed his fingers through his hair backwards and said nothing.

Mr James leaned forwards and gently invited Anthony to tell us why he had done it.

Anthony looked at the head and looked at my dad, then he gave an almighty sniff, said, 'My mum's dead,' and started to cry.

The minute he did that, the grown-ups started to panic. It was like a fire had started. Dad hurried us out of the room, while Mr James kept saying, 'Of course . . . of course . . . of course . . .' Outside the room, he kept pushing us all the way outside, through the millennium garden and into the car park. Anthony carried on sniffing and crying all the way.

In the car park, the lady with the corn rows was just getting out of her car. When she saw me, she smiled. Then she stopped and called after Dad, 'Don't mind me asking, but are these by any chance the boys who . . .'

'Stole money, yeah.'

'Oh. It was stolen, then. I thought the school was just a bit, you know, prosperous. And generous. I was the one who noticed. I'm sorry if it's caused trouble. I just thought . . .'

'You did right. You did right. They stole it. What can you do?'

'At least they gave it to a good cause. I wouldn't have done that at their age. So, you must have done something right.'

'Are you from the Social?'

'Me? No! I'm just a visitor. I go round schools

explaining about the new money and collecting for charity.'

Anthony gave another big sniff. Dad pushed us both into the back of the car and shut the doors. The minute the car door was shut, Anthony turned to me and smiled. He said, 'Result. The old ones are the best ones, eh?'

I wasn't listening. I was watching the lady with the corn rows performing a wonder while alive. She was talking to Dad and he was laughing. Not smiling or doing that polite thing with teeth and air, but actually laughing. And patting his hair down again. He was still smiling when he got back into the car. I leaned forward and asked him what she said.

'She said the pair of you should be locked up.'

We went home over the bridge. I watched all its ribs flicking by through the sunroof. I said, 'Dad, what's a transporter bridge?' He'd definitely mentioned a few bridges in his time – Sydney Harbour, Humber, of Sighs and so on – and I thought it might take him out of himself to talk about some now.

He said, 'Just shut up, for God's sake.'

Which is what St Roch did, so I did it too.

When we got back home, Anthony was worried to hear that the police were returning the money to the Mormons and that we were supposed to go round and apologize to them. Since we hadn't actually stolen the money from the Mormons, this might be a moment of mortal danger and mortification. I mentioned this to Anthony, but it would be unenlightening to write down his reply.

The community policeman came with us to the Latter-day Saints' house and gave them back their money, saying, 'These boys wish to offer their apologies and to return the 3,000 pounds they stole from you.'

The Saints looked at each other.

'You have missed 3,000 pounds?'

The Saints bit their lips.

They should have said no and one of them looked like he was going to, when Dad said, 'It's all right. They've admitted everything.'

'Oh. Well, yes, then and thank you,' said Eli.

'Only you didn't report it,' said the policeman.

'Yes. You know,' said Eli, 'the things of this world and so forth, I think.'

I saw Anthony's eyebrows go up.

'I'd be interested,' said the copper, 'to hear how you came to have so much cash in the house.'

'It was a donation. An anonymous donation.'

'You weren't suspicious about the source of that donation, then?'

'No. Why should we be? We pray a great deal. We thought it was the answer to our prayers.'

'Interesting. It's just that it's been mentioned that you spent 7,000 pounds in cash in Comet a few days back.' He took out a wad of receipts and started to read from them. 'Plasma-screen home cinema, dishwasher, microwave, foot spa . . . Were you praying for these things specifically?'

'We were praying for comfort and encouragement. I think we felt comforted and encouraged.'

'By the dishwasher?'

'And the foot spa.'

So somehow the Saints ended up confirming Anthony's story. Liars don't have a patron saint but they seem to be very good at working together.

On the way home, lots of zebra finches flew right past my nose. The right word for lots of finches is a charm. A charm of zebra finches. Dad had a whole phase on collective terms once. Geese on the ground, for instance, are a gaggle but in the air are a sword, and it's a roister of ravens.

I tried to explain to Anthony the miraculous nature of our escape from earthly tumults in this instance.

He had a different theory. 'It's them. Think about it. We go in there and give them a pile of money and say we nicked it from them. They know we didn't really but they take the money just the same. So that is dodgy. They are dodgy. That's the first point. Second, they've got a house right by the railway line, just where the money was going to be dropped. Is that a coincidence? Or is it something else?'

'Dad bought a house by the railway line. So did everyone else in the street.'

'My dad is not three blokes all wearing identical shirts and talking in a phoney foreign accent, is he? My dad is not dodgy. They are dodgy, as we've established, and they're in the right place. And . . . and . . . they put that camera up. Why?'

'To keep an eye out for burglars.'

'Maybe. Or maybe to keep an eye on us.'

'Why would they want to keep an eye on us?'

'They know someone round here's got the money and they need to know who. They are the gang who stole the money and they're trying to get the missing bag back. It's obvious.'

'Are you sure it's obvious?'

'And now they know we've got it.'

'How?'

'Because we've just given them 3,000 pounds. Duh. They know it's us. They know we've got loads of money we shouldn't have. And now they're going to come after us for it.'

'The Mormons under the leadership of John Doyle Lee massacred 137 poor migrants for entering their territory in 1857. You shouldn't mess with them.'

'That's the whole point. They're not Mormons. They're robbers in disguise.'

'Robbers or Mormons, they're both dangerous. Couldn't we just give them the money?'

'Then we'd know too much. We've got to hide it where they won't find it and then pretend to know nothing about it.'

'Where?'

The answer was obvious. A bank.

The next morning, instead of going to school, we jumped the Widnes bus. The bus driver said, 'No school today?' suspiciously.

Anthony said, 'Dentist.' And he opened his mouth really wide and pointed to his back tooth, saying, 'Look.'

'No thanks. Got enough problems of my own,' said the bus driver.

So now we were playing truant and telling lies in a public place and all for the money.

There were five days left to € Day. All the banks were crowded with people carrying carrier bags, boxes, socks and freezer bags, all stuffed with change, all to be turned into euros. The cashiers poured the coins into weighing machines and then into big bins under the counter. It sounded like being inside a big tin during a hailstorm. The bank clerks were wearing orange earmuffs with little signs on to keep the noise out. It took us half an hour to reach the counter.

'We want to open a bank account,' said Anthony.

'What?' said the woman in the orange earmuffs. Anthony pointed to his ears and she took them off.

'We want to open a bank account.'

'Okey-dokey. Is your mummy with you? Or your dad?'

'No.'

'I really need an adult signature. And some kind of ID.'

Anthony had thought of this, obviously. He gave her his leisure pass from the baths. It had his photograph on and his address, but it wasn't enough. 'You really need to ask your mum to come in.'

'We can't.' Anthony looked her in the eye and said, 'She's dead.'

She looked at him. She looked at me. I tried not to look too sad because I didn't want to contribute to Anthony's errors. But it was hard to look actually happy. And then she did what everyone else always did when we mentioned Mum – she gave us something. An €-shaped money box and two free euros.

We hauled the bag of cash out again. It was heavy and we were nervous that something would happen to it. And that's the thing. We thought the money was going to take care of everything but we ended up taking care of the money. We were always worried about it, tucking it in at night, checking up on it. It was like a big baby. And now we were carrying it round the precinct in a carrycot.

Anthony said, 'I told you we should've bought a house.'

We carried it all the way to Toys 'Я' Us. If Anthony couldn't hide it, he was going to spend it.

We put the cash in a trolley and pushed it down the first aisle. The top end was 'Barbie' so we didn't even slow down. The bottom end was 'Action Man'. Anthony was delighted.

I said, 'A doll by any other name.'

'What?'

'Action Man's a doll.'

'Do *not* start that again.'

'He's in the same aisle as Barbie. Doesn't that tell you something? Look, you can buy clothes for him, like Barbie. And little bags.'

'It's not a bag, it's a tool kit.'

'OK, buy it, then.'

'I don't need it.'

We left the Action Man aisle and went into the Gameboy aisle. There were stacks and stacks of boxes, all plastered with bright monsters and women, their eyes bulging and their arms out. The boxes were noisy to read. I've never seen so many exclamation marks.

Anthony stood scanning them and scanning them. 'We can have any we want,' he said. 'Any. Or all.' Then he said, 'And we don't want any.' He pushed on into weaponry. They had everything – guns, lasers, grenades, knives, spears, swords and mortars. Anthony said, 'If they were real I'd want them.' And moved on. He was getting panicky and quick. 'We're depressed. There must be something here that will cheer us up.'

We were now in a whole aisle entirely full of lunch boxes. There was another aisle full of gel pens that smelt of different fruit. There were over 100 to collect. You could also collect plastic poodles with different hair colours and styles, each with their own birth certificate.

Then Anthony spotted something that he thought was fantastic. It was a castle shaped like a big angry skull. The eyes opened and closed, and when they opened warriors shot out on flying black horses. 'Now that, that is fantastic,' he said. 'Look at that. We've got to have that.' It was 166.99.

We unwrapped it greedily on the grass over in the car park. It was smaller than it looked on the box and it was made of a brittle grey plastic. When you launched the flying warriors, they mostly fell into the skull's nostril. Unless you pressed really hard and then the spring shot out. We tried to fix it but I cut my finger.

'The world is rubbish ,' said Anthony. 'We could have anything in it but everything in it is rubbish.'

On the way home, we binned the castle and stopped at The Carphone Warehouse and bought two video phones and 200 euros' worth of credit each. We put all the credit on them on the bus and rang each other. My ring tone was the theme from *Harry Potter*. It was good that we could see each other's faces on the screen, but we couldn't think of anything to say.

When we got home, something was standing at the bottom of the stairs. It was the bin. 'Hello, Damian. Hello, Anthony,' it said. 'My, my, what a massive bag!'

13

Anthony tried to push the bag behind his back out of sight, which was a bit like trying to push a school behind you out of sight. It was never going to work. And anyway it was pointless, because the bin couldn't actually see. It wasn't the bin who was watching us. I knew who it was. It was the smart lady from school. When I looked at her, she lifted her hand and waved, with just her little finger. I've never seen anyone else do this before or since. It's unique. She said, 'Hello, Damian.'

I said, 'Hello, Bin.'

'Is that really your school bag? You'll give yourself a hernia,' said the smart lady.

For once Anthony was stumped. Luckily, she took his silence for a question. She said, 'The speaker on my bin was broken. Your dad offered to fix it for me.'

'Well, it's fixed now,' said Anthony. And he kept the front door open, as if she was going to leave.

'My name's Dorothy, by the way,' said Dorothy. 'And yes, your dad did a great job.'

She took her coat down from the coat rack. Dad came out of the kitchen, still carrying his screwdriver. He said, 'Oh, you'll stay and have a cup of tea?'

'Well, maybe just a cuppa.'

She followed him into the kitchen with a backward glance at Anthony, who scowled and then hauled the bag upstairs.

In the kitchen Dad put the kettle on and pulled a bag of mince out of the fridge.

She said, 'Couldn't I do a bit of chopping or peeling while I'm waiting for the kettle?'

'No need. Honestly, we know what we're doing,' said Dad.

'I've been living on Pot Noodle for weeks. I just fancy a bit of chopping.'

Dad passed her an onion and a sharp knife. She split the onion in two and gave me half. 'Just do what I do,' she said. She turned her half over so it looked like an igloo, then cut it across the middle and looked at me. I copied her. She said, 'Good.' Then she cut it again, three times. I did the same. She said, 'Good, good, good.' Then she cut the onion into hundreds of tiny pieces, going, 'Good, good, good, good, good, good . . .' and I did the same until we were out of breath.

She looked at Dad and said, 'Pan?'

He said, 'The tea's ready. We'll take over now . . .'

But she'd spotted a pan. She put some oil in it, heated it up and we both dropped handfuls of onions into the oil. She gave me the wooden spoon and said, 'Keep stirring these.' I used to always stir things before we moved house. When everyone had a big craze on porridge, for instance, I used to stir that, and when we were making jelly, I used to stir the cubes in the boiling water until they disappeared. So I had experience.

Dorothy drank her tea and said, 'That was lovely. I suppose I should go now really.'

Dad said, 'I suppose you should stay now really. Since you did practically cook the supper.'

'No. Thanks all the same,' said Dorothy. 'Unless you've got a couple of tins of tomatoes.'

Dad looked puzzled, but he did have some

tins. She put the meat in with the onions and then emptied the tins on top of it. Then she asked for another pan. It took ages to find one, because we only used one and that was just for beans. Then Dad found a whole nest of them, one inside the other. He put them on the side. 'The time has come for us to embrace multi-saucepan-ness in our life.'

Then she wanted milk, then a casserole dish, then cheese, then a cheese grater, then pasta . . .

'Pasta? I'm not sure . . . What exactly are we doing here?' said Dad.

It turned out she was making lasagne from scratch. I had no idea it was so complicated. You can't just go off and watch the television while the oven warms up. The meaty bit is a sauce you make with mince and the tinned tomatoes plus herbs, and you have to let it simmer for a long time to reduce. You could just thicken it if you liked, but reducing makes the flavour more intense.

The white bit is another sauce, which is all in the timing. You make a paste of flour and butter, then very slowly, almost a drop at a time, you add the milk. You have to do it slowly or it goes lumpy. And you have to keep stirring. So I was stirring two pans at once while Dorothy dribbled the milk. Someone rang at the doorbell and she howled, 'Oh, no!' but then we heard Anthony answering it. The last of the milk splashed in and I stirred it with a regular and consistent movement. Dad dropped in the grated cheese. I continued to stir until the cheese was all melted.

Dorothy came and looked over my shoulder and laughed. 'Look at that, not one lump. You could pour that through a sieve. You could drink it from a glass.'

As she bent closer I could smell her hair. It was kind of orangey. Then we heard singing. Anthony had opened the door to carol singers. We all went through and listened to them. It was a family – a mum, a dad, a boy and a girl. The girl was Tricia from Year Five. She gave me a little wave but didn't stop singing.

Dad joined in when they sang 'Silent Night'. I say he joined in. He sang the same song, but not in the same key.

Dorothy laughed and said, 'Do you know "The Holly and the Ivy"?'

Anthony said, 'They don't do requests,' and tried to shut the door on them, but she stopped him and gave them two euros.

Then we ran back into the kitchen and started to

assemble the lasagne. You pour the meat sauce into the oven dish, then pave it with the lasagne. The sauce seeps up through the gaps in the pasta like red moss. Then you pour on the rest of the meat sauce and half the white. Then you pave that. Then you pour on the rest of the white and some grated cheese.

Anthony came in and snarled, 'Why is the kitchen so messy?'

'Because,' said Dad, 'we're cooking in it.'

Anthony said, 'It's not like this when I cook.'

'You don't cook. You warm. And if you feel so strongly about it, you can help clear up while the lasagne is cooking.'

Even Anthony's eyes lit up a little bit when he heard it was lasagne.

I washed the pans. The kitchen started to fill up with lovely, appetizing smells. From inside the oven, you could hear the cheese whistling as it cooked.

I said, 'Pasta's Italian, isn't it? Is this what St Francis would've cooked, then?'

Dad said, 'No. He was from the north. It's rice in the north – risotto and that. Pasta in the south. Also there was no pasta until Marco Polo brought it back from China in 1295. Pasta's a Chinese invention really. It's designer noodles.'

Dorothy said, 'Rubbish. How could pasta be invented by people who don't use forks?'

And Dad went on to explain about forks and how the first person to bring them to England was Thomas à Becket.

I said, 'Thomas à Becket (1118–70), Archbishop of Canterbury, martyred in the cathedral sanctuary.'

'What are you two like? A pub-quiz team, that's what.'

Which is a thing I'd never thought about – that one day I'd be old enough to be in a pub-quiz team with Dad.

'I just know about saints,' I said. 'Dorothy of Cappadocia, died 304, am I right?'

She said she was sure I was. I told her the whole story of how St Dorothy was going to be executed, and how her jailer laughed at her when she said she was going to Heaven. He said, 'Send me some flowers when you get there.' And when he got home his bedroom was filled with roses.

'Why was she going to be executed?'

'She was a virgin martyr.'

'Oh. Right.'

'What exactly is a virgin martyr?'

She said, 'Blimey. The lasagne.'

And we took it out of the oven. It didn't look anything like the frozen ones. It was bubbling and squeaking like it was alive and the cheese sauce had a thick, crackly skin. When we broke into it, a plume of meaty steam rose up from deep inside, like a prayer.

And at that moment Dad finally and unexpectedly told us what the transporter bridge was. It was like a cage and you drove your car into it and then a crane carried it across the river. I didn't say anything, but I stored the moment in my heart. Dad's general knowledge had come back with a vengeance.

'That must've been fantastic,' said Dorothy. 'Like flying in your own car. I think they should bring it back.'

I said, 'Do you by any chance wear a tinted moisturizer?'

Dad said, 'Damian!'

'Leave him alone. If you never ask, you never learn. I do as a matter of fact. It takes a bit of confidence to get up and do what I do. Not in your school. Your school's lovely. But the older ones . . . It's good to have a bit of a mask, you know. It's very clever of you to notice.'

When we'd all finished, Dorothy looked at her

watch and said, 'I'm much later than I planned. But I can't go without helping you to wash up.'

Anthony said, 'No, no. We don't mind washing up. We do it every night. If you've got to go, you . . .'

Dad stopped him. 'Anthony,' he said.

'What?'

Dad looked at him for a second, as if he was trying to work something out, and then he said, 'What *is* in your school bag, by the way? Can't all be homework.'

It could have been a dangerous moment, but Anthony had had time to think now. 'It's sort of homework. It's costumes. For the nativity play.'

Dorothy lit up like a Christmas decoration. 'Nativity play!' she said, 'I haven't seen a nativity play for years. What are you? The kings? Are you going to let us have a look? Go on, go and get them. Give us a treat.'

'No.'

The light went off inside her.

Anthony shrugged, 'You'll spoil the surprise.'

She lit up again. 'Surprise? Are you inviting me to see it?'

Anthony looked like he'd just stepped into a big

mantrap. He said, 'Well, I'm not sure. It's really just for . . .'

'I love a nativity play. I haven't seen one for years. I'll be there. Definitely. As long as you don't mind.'

'First I've even heard of it,' said Dad. 'I get told nothing.'

Anthony looked really cross. He started to clear the table. By the time we'd washed up, it was time for *Who Wants to be a Millionaire?*, which we're always allowed to watch. Dad used to love it, but he never watches it any more. Tonight, though, he sat at one end of the couch. Dorothy sat at the other. And I sat in the middle.

The first contestant looked at the 80,000-euro question and decided to quit, even though Dad was yelling the right answer at the screen.

'You do know, don't you,' said Dorothy, 'that this was filmed a while back. The poor woman is beyond your help now.'

The next contestant was a financial consultant from Bradford with unusually long hair. Disappointingly Dorothy got the 1,000-euro question wrong. I won't embarrass her by repeating it. She said, 'If you ask me, knowledge is overrated.'

The 80,000-euro question was:

Was Dick Turpin hanged in:
a) London
b) York
c) Edinburgh
d) Glasgow?

The financial consultant went 50/50, which really infuriated Dad on the grounds that everyone knows it's York. Dorothy said that even she knew it was York. In the end, even the financial consultant went for York and on to the 160,000-euro question, which was:

After which Catherine is the Catherine wheel named:
a) Catherine of Aragon
b) Catherine of Alexandria
c) Catherine the Great
d) Catherine de Medici?

'I know, I know,' I said.
'How can you know that? How can anyone know that?' said Dorothy, and she turned to Dad. 'Do you know?'

'I think I'd phone a friend and my friend would be this little fella here.' He put his arm round me.

'Catherine of Alexandria (4th century), partly mythical, another virgin martyr and the patron saint of the town of Dunstable in Bedfordshire.'

The financial consultant got it right too. So he was on to the 250,000-euro question, which was:

Who was the first person to play James Bond? Was it:
a) Sean Connery
b) David Niven
c) Roger Moore
d) Robert Holderness?

The man on the telly tried to think it out. He knew that David Niven had been in *Casino Royale* but he wasn't sure if it was the first Bond film. Dad was getting agitated. 'It's a standard pub-quiz question . . .'

Then the man on the telly noticed the last name. He said, 'Bob Holderness. Oh. It was him. It was on the radio. It was on the radio before it was a film and it was him. I'm going for d), Chris.'

'Thank you,' said Dad.

And he played d), and that took him to the 600,000-euro question, which was:

How many lines in a clerihew? Is it:
a) 4
b) 7
c) 5
d) 14?

Dad knew it wasn't 14 (sonnet) or 5 (limerick), so he would've crossed out those two in his head, gone 50/50 and hoped that one of them would still be there, which would give him the right answer.

The consultant just shrugged. 'I've had a great night. Thanks a lot. I'm going to take the money and run.'

Anthony said, 'That's the trouble with this show. People don't realize that you've got to speculate to accumulate.'

'He could have had a go. He had a lifeline left,' groaned Dad.

Dorothy said, 'Why don't you go on it? You'd be a lot less frustrated if you went on it. And not only less frustrated but more rich as well. You'd be a millionaire. You'd have a million pounds.'

Anthony pointed out that it was a million euros now and not a million pounds, so it wasn't worth as much any more. Dorothy said she'd cope with the shortfall somehow.

'But you'd give it all to the water people, anyway, wouldn't you?' I said.

'Me? Fraid not, love. I don't actually work for Water Aid. I work for an agency. I collect for who-ever pays – National Trust in the summer, homeless at Christmas, whatever. If I won a million I'd put it in the bank and never shake a tin again.'

I was surprised and disappointed by this turn of events and would have said something if Dad hadn't said, 'I wouldn't want to be a millionaire. I'd be happy with half. I'd pay off the mortgage, stop having to work extra hours to make ends meet, spend a bit more time with my boys, maybe take them on a nice holiday. Give the rest away.'

I realized then that Dad would make a great millionaire, much better than us, that there he was wishing he could be rich when the house was already stuffed with money and I was suddenly bursting to tell him. But Anthony stood up and said, 'We're supposed to go to bed when *Millionaire*'s over.'

'Go on, then,' said Dad.

'And you're supposed to read us a story.'

Dorothy said, 'I'll get off. I've had a lovely evening . . . but . . .'

Then she and Dad said together, '. . . but this wasn't it!' And they both fell about laughing.

On the way out, she picked up her bin and her coat. There behind it was a big model made of cereal packets. 'Blimey, that's very impressive,' she said.

Anthony shrugged and said, 'Tracy Island. I won a prize for that.'

'I'm not surprised.'

I was surprised. I had no idea how it got there. It was like he'd got so good at lying, the Weetabix boxes believed him.

I went to Anthony's bedroom window so I could watch Dad and Dorothy saying goodbye. Anthony was lying on his bed. 'Come and see,' I said. Dad was holding the car door open for her.

'Don't want to.'

'Come on. She's good.'

'She is not good.'

'The lasagne was good.'

'No, it wasn't. My mum's lasagne was good. That lasagne was rubbish. It didn't even have sweetcorn in it.'

There's no point talking to him when he's like

this, so I just listened to her engine starting up. Then I heard Dad slapping the roof of her car as it moved off. She pipped her horn softly. I was going to go then, but Anthony snarled at me, 'Why is it always me? Why do you leave everything to me?'

'What?'

'You found the money. Why don't you ever help?'

'What are you talking about?'

'The minute we walked in she was staring at the bag. Just staring at it. Like an X-ray machine and what did you do?'

'I said hello.'

'You said nothing. It was me who did the talking. I had to make up that thing about the nativity play and she said, "I'll have to come and see it."'

'It'll be nice.'

'Damian, we're not *in* the nativity play. Remember?'

'Oh, yeah.'

'And she knew we were lying. And who had to make up the lie? Me? And who'll have to get us into the play now? Me. And who went upstairs and hid the money in the Subbuteo box?'

'Did you?'

'Yes, I did. And then what happened? Someone was at the door. Did you answer it? No, I did. And who was there?'

'Carol singers.'

'Carol singers. It was Tricia with the Tracy Island thing.'

'I did wonder how that got there.'

'And her dad and her brother. And she'd told them that we had loads of money. And they were asking for some.'

'What did you say?'

'He said the VAT were going to close his business down if he didn't give them three grand by tomorrow, so could I give him three grand.'

'And did you?'

'If I gave him the money, he'd know it was all true and what would happen then? Millions of people all wanting three grand knocking at the door day and night.'

'So you said no.'

'I couldn't, could I? *She* came out of the kitchen. I had to get rid of them. I told them I'd give them the money if they pretended to be carol singers. I gave them three grand. She gave them two euros.'

'It's good that they're not closing his business, though.'

'It's not good, Damian. None of this is good. Have you thought about this? Everyone knows we've got money, right? So soon everyone is going to start wondering where we got it from. And that's when the police will get involved. Have you thought about that?'

'No. I haven't.'

'Well, luckily I have. I told them we won it on the scratch cards.'

'That's good.'

'And her, she knows. She knew they weren't carol singers. All that, *do you know "The Holly and the Ivy"* stuff. She was trying to catch them out. That's why I said, "They don't do requests," and shut the door.'

I could see he was tired and worried. 'You're cleverer than me, that's what it is. You're just cleverer . . .'

Suddenly the room was filled with a cold, blue light. I thought it might be a bit of a vision, so I pretended not to notice. But Anthony could see it too. He said, 'Cops. Look.'

There were two police cars down in the road below. They had big black numbers painted on their roofs. One was 9 and one was 23. Anthony said these were so the police helicopter could tell which car was which.

Dad came in. 'There's been a burglary,' he said.

I gasped, 'Is it us?'

He looked surprised. 'Why would it be us? You daft thing.' He ruffled my hair, while Anthony kicked me discreetly on the shins.

'Hang on, though,' said Dad.

The community policeman was walking over to ours. Dad went down and opened the door to him. We leaned over the banister and listened. Someone had burgled the Mormons.

'I didn't like to mention it in their current state of distress,' said the community copper, 'but we could all do with a cup of tea.'

'Oh, sure,' said Dad.

'And toast if it's going.'

'No problem.'

Anthony said we should sneak down and follow them into the kitchen.

'What for?'

'Because we won't be able to hear them once the kettle starts.'

'What do we want to hear them for?'

'Intelligence and surveillance, obviously.'

The kettle was incredibly loud actually. I hadn't

noticed it before. The community copper was saying, 'I suppose if someone had to be burgled at this time of year, it was best it was them. They don't actually celebrate Christmas, I believe. So it's not spoiling much for them.'

'Is that right?' said Dad. 'And they'd just bought all that new stuff. The dishwasher and that. I suppose they left the boxes out for the bin men and someone spotted them.'

'It's a possibility. There again, they didn't take the dishwasher. Or the telly. Or the DVD player. Very unusual. They've turned the place over but they don't seem to have taken anything. They seem to have been looking for something.'

'Like what?'

'Spiritual comfort and encouragement, I suppose. Anyway, their being done improves the odds on the rest of you *not* being done, statistically, so that's a comfort. Two sugars for me and I don't know about the CID.'

Dad helped him carry the tea out to the crime scene. Anthony tried to follow him, but Dad sent us back to bed.

'Come on,' he said, 'show's over. Off you go.'

Anthony came into my room. He said, 'Hear what

he said? The burglars were looking for something. You know what that was, don't you? The money. The train robbers are looking for their money and they know it's round here somewhere. They saw that lot buying all kinds of stuff and assumed they had it.'

'You said the Mormons *were* the train robbers yesterday.'

'New evidence, Damian. Like they've just been burgled. How can they be the robbers if they've just been robbed.'

'So who are the robbers, then?'

'Obviously, it's Dorothy.'

'No. Obviously it's not Dorothy.'

'Think about it. You put thousands in her bin. Does she give it to charity? No, she tells the head. Why? Because she wants to know who put it there. Which is you, idiot. Then when she's found out, does she go home? No, she hangs around the school, getting pally with Dad. Why? So she can find out where we live. The next thing, she's wandering round our house like she owned it, rooting around in our kitchen and all that. Why? So she can check up on us and find out where the money is. The next thing you know, the neighbours get burgled.'

Now I could see Anthony was passionate in his belief, but I could also see that he was mistaken. 'Anthony, if she knew *we* had the money, why would she burgle the house next door and not us?'

'I don't know. A communication problem, probably. She's not on her own, is she? It's a big organization. There's dozens of them. And they're everywhere and they all know and they're all after us. And not just them. Everyone who hears about the money wants it. But it's OK . . .' He didn't look OK. He looked like he was going to cry. 'What we're going to do. We're going to hide it in your den.'

'It's not a den. It's a hermitage.'

'Whatever. We're going to hide it there and take a wedge each . . .'

'What if someone looks there?'

'Like who? No one else knows about it. Do they?'

'The man with the glass eye.'

It took him a while, but eventually he managed to repeat, 'The man with the glass eye?'

'He had a look inside the day we . . .' I didn't go on. Anthony looked like he was going to cry. 'Anthony, let's tell Dad. He had really good ideas about what to do with it and . . .'

'You don't understand a thing, do you? We can't trust anyone.'

'But Dad . . .'

'Dads and mums are no different. One minute they're there and the next they're gone. You should know that. We're on our own, Damian. Get used to it.'

By the time I'd thought of something to say back to him, he'd gone to bed. He was curled up in a ball deep under the sheets, pretending to be asleep.

14

Next morning, Anthony shovelled all the money out of the Subbuteo box and into our school bags. 'We're going to have to keep it with us. All the time. No days off. If we leave it in the house, it'll get burgled or she'll find it. We can't put it in your den. We can't put it in the bank. We'll have to keep it with us. Maybe we should stay off sick?'

'But we're not sick.'

'No good anyway. They're casting for the nativity play today. We've got to get parts or our cover's blown.'

So we put the bags of cash on our backs. To be

metaphorical about it, the money had become a burden.

There was a man outside putting up a sign that said, 'This is a Homewatch Area.' Dad said it was pretty ironic putting it up on the day after the burglary. We set out for school.

Terry from IT was getting into his car. He pointed to the sign and said, 'Irony, eh? Do they still do irony at school? If they ask you for an example, that's it.'

'OK. Will do,' said Anthony, and walked on.

When we were crossing the field, I said, 'What if we don't get picked? For the nativity play?'

'We'll get picked, don't worry.'

When we were at All Saints Primary, everyone wanted to be in the nativity play because you got a special party of your own afterwards. It turned out to be different at Great Ditton. When Mr Quinn came in and said, 'Right 5M, this class is going to provide Mary, Joseph and the shepherds for the juniors' nativity play. Who wants to be Joseph?' I shot my hand up in the air, the same as anyone would. But when I looked around, instead of being surrounded by waving arms, I was on my own. Not one other boy had put his hand up. They were all sitting there looking at me. I couldn't understand it. Then I looked closer and saw that every one of them was clutching a twenty-pound note under their desks. Anthony had paid them all off.

Mr Quinn looked uncomfortable, 'No one else?'

I kept my hand up there.

'No one else want to be St Joseph? Damian could be a shepherd. He's probably had enough of saints, eh? Jake, what about you?'

'Couldn't do it, sir. Allergy, sir.'

'Allergy to what?'

'Synthetics, sir.'

Mr Quinn looked puzzled.

'The beard.'

I kept my hand high up through all of this, so he had to pick me in the end.

Trying the costume on was interesting. I'd always endeavoured to emulate the saints but I'd never actually dressed like one before. I had sandals, a crook and a big black beard.

Mr Quinn helped me put them on. He said, 'St Joseph never did anything weird, did he? I mean, he didn't spurt milk or levitate or anything?'

'Not unless being visited by angels is weird.'

He looked me searchingly in the eye and then said, 'No, no. I can live with that.'

Anthony was playing one of the kings. His teacher (Miss Nugent) said, 'Now there are three kings – Melchior, Caspar and Balthasar. Which d'you want to be?'

'The one with the gold.'

The one with the gold was Melchior, by the way.

Miss Nugent made Anthony a block of gold out of a Rockport shoebox wrapped up in gold paper. He carried that block of gold with him everywhere. He became interested and inspired by historical aspects of the nativity story. For instance, he said to me, 'Do you realize how much a block of gold that big would be worth at today's prices? A lot. An awful lot. It makes you wonder.'

'What?'

'Well, he had all this money and then later on, when he was grown up, he was poor. They must've spent it. They must've had a great time.'

We had a big dress rehearsal. We didn't go home after school. We all took sandwiches and waited in class for our turn to see the make-up lady, which was Tricia's mum. There were dozens of little girls dressed as angels. They had to stand in the corridor and practise 'Silent Night' and 'Little Donkey' until they sounded like real angels. Miss Nugent kept giving them orange squash. I know they weren't really angels but they still made me feel safer.

Tricia's mum drew lines on my face with an eyebrow pencil to make me look old and she made my hair grey with flour. And I was ready to go on.

I'd already managed to Google up quite a lot about St Joseph. I think Miss Nugent found it all very useful. For instance, when it was my turn to knock on the inn door, she said, 'Remember now, Damian. Be tired. St Joseph has walked a long way. So he's very tired.'

I said, 'Well, he was a carpenter, so he was very fit. And the walk from Nazareth, well, people did walks like that all the time. It would've been like taking a bus to them. Also, she was going to have a baby. So they weren't exactly planning to sleep. They might have been stressed, but I wouldn't have said tired.'

You could see she was impressed by the way she said, 'Whatever,' and went straight on to the three kings.

When I came off, Tricia's mum said my beard

was too tight. 'The elastic's making your ears go red. See if you can fix it yourself.'

I went to the boys' toilets to try and loosen it in the mirror. There was a man already in there with a huge black beard and a big wooden staff.

'St Joseph,' I said, 'dates unknown.'

'I just had to say, you're doing a great job.'

'Thanks very much. I'm not making you sound too stressed?'

'No. I was stressed. The way you're playing it, it really puts me back in there.'

'Thanks.'

'Do you want me to take you through the birth, because obstetrics has really changed?'

'I think we're going to skip that bit.'

'OK. Well, break a leg.'

In the corridor, Mr Quinn said, 'What about the bag, Damian? You're not going to be carrying that round with you on the night, I hope?'

I'd got so used to the bag, I'd forgotten it was there. If I couldn't carry it, where could I put it? I looked at Anthony. He just shrugged.

'What are you wearing it for anyway?' said Mr Quinn.

I looked at Anthony again. He looked at me pleadingly.

Mr Quinn said, 'You don't need it, do you?'

He was coming towards me. He was going to take it off me. I blurted out, 'My mum's dead.' He took a step backwards immediately. Raised his hands and said, 'OK. I'm sure St Joseph was carrying a lot of stuff with him on the day. Why don't you go and practise with Dave?'

Dave was the donkey. He was made of plywood and fun fur. He stood on a platform with castors on it and he had a pair of sacking saddlebags stuffed with straw. I took him out in the corridor and practised pulling him up and down with Mary (Rebecca Knowles) on his back. It took a while, but I eventually got the knack of steering him. We powered up and down the lino, doing three-point turns by the fire doors.

Rebecca kept saying, 'I will be the Mother of God,' over and over, and we could hear the angels practising 'It was on a Starry Night' in Miss Nugent's class, and I wished that I could live my whole life inside a nativity play.

That night, I was still humming 'It was on a Starry Night' when I went up to bed. There was going to be a collection for Water Aid after the play. The angels were supposed to give out envelopes before and collect them again afterwards. I managed to get hold of a whole packet of envelopes. I lay on the floor putting a twenty-pound note in each one. I was planning to put them in a bag and hand them to the Angel Gabriel.

Suddenly a big leather sandal stood on the envelopes. There was a huge hairy foot in it. I looked up. Above me was a brown robe with a massive man inside. Round his waist was a belt with seven chunky iron keys dangling from it. I sat up and hit my head on the biggest one. The big man said a swearword. I won't say which one as it was unenlightening. And then he said, 'Don't put your address on the back of them. They pass it on to other charities.'

I said, 'St Peter (d. 64)?'

He just swore again. 'Don't remind me. It wasn't the nicest way to go. Put your address on the back of there, you'll be besieged. I promise you. Every tin-shaker in Christendom will be on your doorstep. Believe me, I know what I'm talking about. I'm infallible.'

I actually had written our address on some of the envelopes, but only a few.

'Is this yours?' He was holding up a key.

It was the key to the old house. I normally kept it on the windowsill.

'Jointed pin tumbler. Engineering perfection that. The drum action is miraculous. I'm the patron saint of keys, you know. About this money . . .'

'It's stolen.'

'I know. I am the patron saint of keys and locks and security arrangements in general. I know it's hot.'

'Doesn't that mean we should give it back? But if we do, they'll burn it. So that's bad too, isn't it? I keep trying to do good but everything's messed up.'

'You're stressed. I'm stressed. We're all stressed. This is my portfolio, right – like I said, keys, locks, security. On top of that – fishermen, popes, Rome . . . I am run off my (swear) feet. I'm supposed to mind the gate too, you know. I see everyone in and everyone out.'

'Do you really? Everyone?'

'Yeah. Why? Was there someone you were looking for?'

I said, 'Well . . .' and then I changed my mind. I said, 'No. It doesn't matter.'

He looked at me and sat on the end of the bed. 'I'm going to tell you something now I've never mentioned to anyone. Didn't mention it to Luke or

Mark or John when they were asking. Just kept it to myself. But . . . it's true. Are you listening?'

And then he told me the story of the feeding of the 5,000. I didn't like to say it was fairly well documented and widely known. He talked about all the people following Jesus and listening to him and how Jesus never planned anything, and how every time Jesus got hungry he acted like this was a completely unexpected development. 'He wouldn't put a scarf in his pocket if he was climbing Everest,' he said. 'And he definitely didn't bring a picnic for these people. The police said there were 5,000, but I reckon there was twice that number, easy. And they were all starving. D'you know what he did?'

'Well . . .' I didn't want to spoil his story but I had to admit, 'Five loaves and two fish.'

'No. You see. I knew you'd say that. That's what everyone said afterwards and I'll tell you why they said it – guilt.'

'Sorry. What?'

'A little kid came up to him – about your size. His name was – I've forgotten. I still see him sometimes. Anyway, he came up with these loaves and sardines and Jesus blessed them and passed them round. He wasn't trying to do a miracle, he was just one of those people who thought everything would be all right, you know. Anyway, so he passed these sardines, and the first person he passed them to passed them on. Know why? Because he had a honey cake and a piece of lamb hidden in his purse. So he passed the fish on and sneaked the honey cake out and made out he'd just taken it off the plate. And the next person, he had a pocket full of dates, so he did the same – sneaked one out, passed the plate on. And so it went on. The truth was, every single one of them had food with them, but they were all keeping it to themselves. Hidden away. Every one of them looking after Number One. And they would have starved where they stood rather than let anyone see. But as the plate came round with the loaves and the fish on, they all got their own food out and started to eat and, as they ate, they started to share and then it began, the biggest pic-nic in history. And the plate went all the way round back to Jesus and this kid – I'll think of his name in a minute – and it still had the fish and the loaves on. And Jesus was a bit taken aback, but when he looked up (he'd been talking all the time) he could see that everyone was eating. So he said, "What happened?" and I just said, "A miracle." Because I didn't want to bad-mouth anyone in front of him. I was always bad-mouthing people and he hated it and it was turning into a nice evening. And at the time he didn't say anything, and I thought I'd fooled him, but now I see it was a kind of miracle. The best kind. Because all those people had all they needed. Except something – I don't know what you'd call it – courage, maybe, or grace. And then this little kid. He stood up and suddenly everyone there got bigger. They were all filled with it and they were there for hours, talking and laughing and drunk on this stuff – this grace or whatever. A little kid stood up and was ready to be generous and that's all it took. One little kid. He wasn't planning to save the world. He was planning lunch. He just did the right thing at the right time. One little kid and a plate of fish, and 5,000 people sorted. And that's according to the police. Like I said, it was twice that, easy. Do you understand what I'm talking about?'

'A bit.'

'I'm talking about you.'

'Now I'm really lost.'

'Look, I can't say too much. Because there's free will and all that to think about, but I will say this. See this key . . .'

It was the key to our old house.

'Miracle of the lockmaker's art, this. See it? Keep it with you. Keep it safe. I think I can say that without going too far. Keep it with you. Keep it safe.'

15

It was the big night. We all had to go round on tip-toe backstage so that no one could hear us. Anthony and I looked out through the curtains. The hall was full of parents, all perched on tiny chairs, nearly all pointing video cameras. At the back we could see Dad trying to squeeze past everyone to get into some spare seats. Dorothy was with him.

'What did he have to bring her for?' asked Anthony.

'You invited her,' I reminded him.

Then it began. An angel from Year Four came and told me about Mary having the baby. Then we set off for Bethlehem, with all the other angels at the front of the stage singing 'Little Donkey'. When we got to the far side of the stage we were hidden by the curtains. Mary got off and sneaked behind the inn, back to stage left, but Dave the donkey wouldn't fit so I had to go out the side door, run through the foyer, dragging the donkey past the head's office, and back in through the dining-hall doors.

St Joseph was waiting. He said, 'That was terrific. You really put me back in there. Look . . . tears.'

'Thanks. I mean, sorry if I upset you, but . . .'

'No, no, catharsis, that's what it's all about.'

'OK. Got to go. Got a cue.'

I was heading for the stage when Dave snagged on something. I looked back and there he was. The man with the glass eye had grabbed the donkey's tail. I caught my breath.

He spoke very, very quietly. 'You remember me, don't you?'

I nodded.

'I'm the poor man.'

I nodded again.

'I think you've got some more money for me, haven't you?'

He looked over my head at the bag. I tried to move round so he wouldn't see it. But he'd already spotted it. He reached out towards me. But the door behind him opened and all the angels came giggling out, followed by Miss Nugent.

'Come on, Damian,' she hissed. 'You should be in Bethlehem by now.'

Glass Eye pulled back behind the locker, away from me and the bag. He didn't want anyone to see him.

'Damian! Come on!' pleaded Miss Nugent.

I looked at Glass Eye and mimed, 'Got to go,' and went. Simple as that. I headed for the stage, surrounded by angels.

When I was back behind the curtain, Miss Nugent said, 'And what on earth are you doing with that anachronistic bag on your back? Did they have Nike in the first century? I don't think they did, did they?'

I didn't know what to do. But Mr Quinn was there, to work the star of wonder (it was on a pulley). He said quietly, 'I did tell him it was all right, Miss Nugent . . .' and then he whispered something to her. She rolled her eyes but went off to play the piano.

The angels had to sing 'Little Donkey' again before me and Rebecca went back on. So I just had time to do one clever thing. Here's what I did: I took all the straw out of the saddlebags and stuffed the money into them. Then I put the straw in my own school bag. I switched the money and the straw.

Then I went up to Mr Quinn and gave him my bag. He looked very surprised (and pleased). I said, 'I don't need it after all. Shall I take it to the cloakroom?'

He said, 'Well, that's great. No. I'll take it back for you. Well done, Damian. Moving on, eh?' And he ruffled my hair and took the bag.

I watched it go.

Then it was our turn to go on and knock at the doors of all the inns and ask if they had any room. It was the same door three times but a different innkeeper each time.

'Have you any room?'

'No, we're fully booked. Don't you know there's a census on?'

I could just see Glass Eye standing behind Dad. I turned my back to the audience – which you're not supposed to do – so that he could see I'd taken my bag off.

'Have you any room?'

'Not for the likes of you. Take that mangy donkey away from my hotel at once.'

I heard the fire door thud quietly as I knocked at the third inn door. I knew he'd gone off to look for the bag. He'd find it in the cloakroom. If he looked inside he'd see it was full of straw. What would he do then? Probably kill me.

'Have you any room?' I said, a bit faster than usual. 'My wife is having a baby.'

'Not really, but if you're stuck you could bed down in the stable. It's dry and warm at least.'

We went through the inn door. Rebecca said, 'Oh, I thank you.' Everyone said, Aaaaah. And camera flashes went off like sparklers. We sneaked behind the curtain.

Mr Quinn started yanking on the pulley to make the star of wonder cross the stage. The kings were supposed to follow it, singing 'We Three Kings'. After the third verse (the one about myrrh) we were supposed to go back on. Except I had other plans. I was going to disappear with the money.

The singing started, 'We Three Kings of Orient are . . .' I had three verses before anyone noticed I wasn't there. Three verses till I missed my cue. It was a three-verse head start.

The saddlebags with the money in were really heavy, so I just left them where they were, on the back of the donkey, and pulled the donkey after me down the corridor. I was going to go straight for the main doors. But I'd forgotten that all the angels were out in the corridor. I had to go the other way, past the head's office and the cloakrooms. That's where the bags were. Glass Eye might be there. I walked slowly, listening. The kings were already on to 'Gold I bring . . .' There, on the floor of the cloakroom, was my empty school bag and a pile of straw next to it. He'd already looked in the bag. He'd already know I'd tried to trick him. He'd already be looking for me.

I didn't have time to change so I grabbed my coat from the hook and put it on over the St Joseph costume so I wouldn't look so noticeable. Then I trundled the donkey off towards the main door. I froze. Mr Quinn was outside, smoking a cigarette. The kings were on 'Frankincense to offer have I . . .' Fancy Mr Quinn smoking. He must know it's bad for you. Suddenly he dropped the cigarette, came inside and headed for the main hall. I dragged the donkey after me, out of the big doors, bouncing it down the steps, and ran across the car park. I was going so fast it nearly fell over on its side.

As I passed the school gates, I looked back. There was no sign of Glass Eye. He wasn't after me yet. I legged it over the road and into the bus shelter. Miraculously, a Smart Bus was coming. There were a few people sitting up on the top deck. Their faces were all lit up in the square bus windows. They looked down on me like choirs of angels. I grabbed the saddlebags and climbed on board, leaving the donkey in the bus shelter.

I asked for a single to Smithdown Road. It was seventy-five pence. Then I realized that though I had thousands of pounds hanging over my shoulder, I didn't have any change. I didn't have anything smaller than a tenner. The bus driver just stared at me and said, 'Seventy-five pence,' again.

I patted the pockets of my coat. I didn't want to open the saddlebags in case all the money fell out.

'Can I sit down a minute? I think . . .'

'You've come out in your costume,' said the driver. 'And your money's in your kecks.'

I didn't want to lie. Not when I was dressed as St Joseph, so I just said, 'Sorry.'

'Sing me "Little Town of Bethlehem" and I'll let you off,' said the driver as he pulled out.

I sat in the front seat and very quietly started singing. In the wing mirror, I could see the donkey's head sticking out of the bus shelter, like out of a stable. I couldn't see anyone following me. 'The hopes and fears of all the years are met in thee tonight,' I sang.

After all this was over, Dad told me what happened during the play. When it was time for my entrance, Mary came on but obviously I didn't. She sat by the manger with nothing happening. Then she said, in a big loud voice, 'This is nice and cosy, Joseph.' She thought I was just behind the set. When I still didn't come on, she said it again, only louder: 'This is nice and cosy, Joseph.' People started to giggle. My dad said he started to fret. I bet Glass Eye was fretting too, standing at the back. He was probably just about to go out after me. Mary went, 'I SAID THIS IS NICE AND . . .' and then she stopped. Someone did come on. It wasn't me but it was someone with a big beard and robes and – this was what Dad said – a kind of glow. Everyone had been leaning forward but now everyone sat back in their chairs, like they were relaxing in front of a nice fire. Dad said it must have been Mr Quinn who'd quickly wrapped a blanket round himself and put a tea towel on his head. 'He must have used one of those sticks you have when you go camping. You know, you snap them and they glow. Just like that. It was very effective. You couldn't see his face properly, but he had this aura. I forgot to worry about you for a minute.' I knew when he said that that it wasn't Mr Quinn at all. It was the real St

Joseph who had stood in for me so that even Glass Eye had to just stay and watch him. So thanks for that.

I got off the Smart on Smithdown Road and walked back down Panama Street for the first time since we left. A bizarrely bright star was shining straight through the tiny gap in the houses, lighting up the door of number 37. I put the key in the door, turned it like I used to and stepped inside.

Obviously I knew the house would be empty. I had helped empty it and no one had bought it. I knew it would be empty. I just didn't know it would be that empty. It was the emptiest place I'd ever been. It was like waking up in the morning a bit late, hurrying downstairs and then discovering that the stairs had gone, that you'd stepped off into space. That's what it was like, space.

It didn't even sound like our house. It sounded like a submarine. And when I started up the stairs, with the saddlebags, it sounded like a giant drumming on the side of a submarine. I hurried to the landing and opened the airing-cupboard door. There were no towels or sheets inside, the way there used to be. But there was a long steel pole with a hook on the end, hanging on the back of the door. This was a special pole for opening the loft and pulling down the easy-store telescopic loft ladder. I took the pole and stood under the loft hatch. I tweaked the catch. The door dropped open and smacked the wall. The telescopic ladder rattled down, sounding like 10,000 tin parachutists hitting a corrugated roof. Then it stopped suddenly, the bottom rung swinging in mid-air just above my head. I touched the catch to release the lower half and another 10,000 tin parachutists landed. Then it went quiet.

I hauled the saddlebags up into the loft. I'd never been up there. I'd seen Dad go up and down from time to time. I'd always wanted to know what was up there. Nothing. Even more nothing than in the rest of the house. Nothing and a big grey metal tank full of water. Every now and then you could hear a pinging drip of water. But that was all. There was a space between the tank and the wall. I pushed the saddlebags into the gap and went back down the ladder.

I was just pushing the lower half of the ladder back up when I heard it. There was someone at the front door. I held my breath. It was OK. They couldn't get in. I remembered what St Peter said about the key and slid my hand into my pocket to make sure it was still there. It wasn't. I'd left it in the front door. I could hear it turning in the lock now. I raced back up the ladder and hauled it up after me. When I reached down to pull the hatch back up, I could hear someone coming up the stairs. I quickly pulled the hatch back into place and scrabbled over to the water tank, holding my breath. They were walking round right underneath me now, who-ever they were. I tried to slide myself into the gap between the tank and the wall.

Suddenly the tank shook and thundered. Water poured out of it and into it like it was going to explode. I scurried away from it. Someone down-stairs had flushed the toilet. I tried to control my breathing, which is probably what gave me the hic-cups. I hiccuped once. Couldn't believe it. Listened hard. The footsteps downstairs stopped. They'd heard – or thought they'd heard – something and now they were listening properly. I held my breath. There were voices and more footsteps. I hiccuped again. The footsteps stopped again. I pulled my St Joseph beard out of my pocket and put it over my mouth to stifle the noise. That's when I heard the *Harry Potter* theme playing very close by. I looked around. The video mobile. The video mobile was in my coat pocket and now it was ringing. It was too late to do anything about it. Before I could even switch it off, the hatch of the loft dropped open. A cube of light punched into the loft. The telescopic ladder pitched up on its end, nearly hitting me in the jaw. It clattered down. Then stopped mid-air and swinging. Then someone undid the catch and it hit the floor. Then there was a moment of quiet. Then someone stepped on the bottom rung. I sat shaking, watching the top of the ladder quiver under the weight of somebody's feet. Another step. Another quiver. No word. I hiccuped again. Then there were two steps very quick, one after the other. I tried to back into the shadow. Then the ladder shook again. A hand reached into the space. Then I saw the back of a man's head. Then I screamed and screamed and screamed and screamed. Then the man turned to face me. And it was Dad.

'What the hell are you doing up there, you daft bat?'

To be confessional about it, I did actually cry. He pulled me over and carried me down the ladder. I couldn't breathe properly. He kept hold of me and didn't say anything for a while but, 'Hush.' He walked into my old bedroom and whispered in my ear, 'Remember in here? This is your old room, eh? Come on, just get your breath.' I was trying to, but every time I started to feel calmer this horrible mixture of crying and hiccups kicked off again. He took me into the next room. 'And this was mine and, you know, hers,' he said. We went over to the bay window and stood looking out.

'The day we moved out, I saw you take the key. When you were gone after the play, we went home to see if you were there. I noticed the key was missing from your windowsill. So . . . here we are, eh?'

Anthony held up his video phone. 'I was worried about you, so I rang you,' he said. 'Could you not see me on the screen?'

'The phone was in my coat pocket.'

Dad stared at the video phone. 'Would someone mind telling me what is going on?' he said.

I looked at Anthony. I knew I couldn't do this any more. He nodded his head. I said, 'There's a bag behind the water tank.'

Dad went up and got the saddlebags. They didn't close properly. So he was just about to step back on the ladder when he saw what was inside. He said something unenlightening. Then he said, 'Where the hell did this come from?'

'It just fell out of the sky. I thought it was from God.'

'From God? Why would God give you . . .' He looked into the bag.

'There were 229,370 old pounds,' said Anthony. 'What's left is still valid for twenty-two hours.'

'Blimey.' He looked at the pile of money. 'And you really thought you could keep it?'

The way he said it, it sounded obvious that we'd just made a mistake, like making pastry instead of cake.

We looked at each other.

'You daft pair,' he said. 'Come on.'

'What're you going to do?'

'Hand it in, of course.'

'Will we get into trouble?'

'Not at all. They were only going to burn it anyway. They'll be very pleased with you.'

He ruffled my hair.

Anthony said, 'Will we get a reward, then?'

'Get in the car,' laughed Dad, and he drove us home through town and opened the sunroof, so we could lie on the seat and watch the Christmas lights passing over our heads.

There were some fat white angels, and some red and green bells, and some words like 'Peace on Earth' and 'Goodwill to Men', and I thought, Of course Dad would make everything all right

again. And I didn't even mind that the illuminated Santa Clauses looked nothing like the real St
Nicholas. And when we got home, who was waiting
at the door but Dorothy? It all felt like a big, happy
ending.

But it wasn't the ending. And it wasn't happy.

16

It's not unusual to have a bad Christmas. Even on the first Christmas, King Herod heard about another king being born in a stable and he thought it must be a plot against him, so he spent the whole time fretting. Which wasn't exactly relaxing. And when he'd worried about it for a while, he decided that the safest thing for him to do was to send his soldiers to kill all the newborn boys in Judaea. So that year the baby boys of Judaea had an even worse Christmas than Herod did.

Jesus got away, obviously. Even though statistically it was really his fault that the others died. They were collateral damage, like the people who were killed by the fatal flying splinters at the execution of St Catherine. It's amazing how many people get hurt just by being in the wrong place at the wrong time.

Dad was pleased and surprised that Dorothy was waiting on the doorstep. He flashed his headlights and pipped the horn. But in the headlights, I saw her face. She was biting her lip and looking worried. Dad parked up and got out. Anthony hissed, 'He'd better not tell her. And *you'd* better not tell her either.'

When I got out of the car, Dorothy was holding Dad's hand. She put her other hand out for me to hold. I could smell her orangey shampoo again. She was saying, 'I just came by, you know, and the front door was open. I never thought for a minute . . . I'm so sorry. I did call them right away.'

We'd been burgled. The front door was splintered round the lock. The Christmas tree was flat on the floor, in a litter of broken baubles and tangled tinsel. It looked like it had been hit by a tornado. The presents were squashed. The ceramic coals from the living-flame gas fire were all over the place. In the kitchen, the cupboards had all been emptied on to the floor, as had the rubbish from the bin for some reason. Dad sat down and just stared at the mess.

He was still staring when the community police officer arrived. 'You've not been burgled. You've been ransacked,' he said, and wrote a number down on a piece of paper. 'You give that to your insurance company and make a claim. Obviously they can't really recompense you for this. They can't give you your Christmas back. It'll probably be next Christmas by the time you get the cheque.'

Dad just sat there staring.

Dorothy had made a pot of tea. 'I couldn't think what else to do,' she said.

The community policeman said, 'Well, you could do a bit of toast.'

'Oh. Sorry.'

'They've given it a right old going-over, haven't they? The strange thing is, they haven't taken that much. It's more like they were looking for something. Is there anything they should be looking for?'

Dad just carried on staring.

'Only we've had reports about one of these bags of sterling being missing in the area, which might explain this spate of robberies. Not that they can do anything with it now anyway. The banks have all been warned to report any large deposits and they've only got a day before it all turns into waste paper.'

Then he went. Dad never said goodbye, never got up. Just sat there staring at the tree. Now that I came to notice it, so did Anthony. It was Dorothy who saw the policeman out. When she came back she said, 'I was collecting once for War on Want, CAFOD maybe, one of them. At the NEC in Birmingham. They had Nelson Mandela talking for them. Did my job for me. Couldn't sign up the standing orders fast enough afterwards. D'you know what he said? He said, "The only wealth is life." What d'you think of that? He said money can be a prison just like, you know, no money. The only wealth is life. Which you've got plenty of . . . You've got each other, got a place, got your health. Life. Everything else is a disappointment. Like the Great Wall of China.'

I looked at her. So did Anthony. The Great Wall of China?

'Surely you know.' She shrugged. 'It's not really made of china at all.'

I snorted. Anthony snorted. Dad looked up. She bit her lip. He started laughing. And he carried on laughing until I joined in and I carried on until

Dorothy joined in and finally even Anthony was laughing.

Then Dad stood up and went out to the car. Anthony went after him. He said, 'Dad, don't. Please, Dad, please don't.' But it was obvious he was going to. He strode back in with the donkey's saddlebags and dropped them down on the dining table.

'What's that?'

Dad picked them up and shook them so all the great lumps of money fell out like bricks from a hod. Dorothy gasped. Anthony groaned, then took himself off to bed.

'Where did that . . . Is that yours?'

'This is what they were looking for,' said Dad.

Dorothy touched the bag of money gently, like she was worried it might explode. 'You know what I said about the only wealth is life? Well . . . this is the life.'

He laughed again, but it wasn't a happy laugh. 'They took our Christmas. We'll take their cash.'

And that was the first time I realized he was going to keep it.

'But you can't keep it. That would be stealing.'

'If you steal something, you have to steal *from* someone. Who would you be stealing from?'

'The government.'

'Well, obviously this is between you three,' said Dorothy, 'but you do know – I'm just saying – you do know the government was planning to burn this?'

Dad jumped on that. 'Yeah. Burn it! When there are poor people everywhere. Why couldn't they just give it to the poor? That would've been better, wouldn't it?'

Anthony had explained that to me already. 'Well, it's to do with the money supply. You see, the way it works . . .'

'All right, all right, I know how it works. I'm making a point.'

'Which is?'

'That we are going to take this into town tomorrow, change it for euros and spend it.'

The doorbell rang. Dad and Dorothy looked at each other in fright and started to shovel the money back into the bags.

I went to the door. 'Not yet,' hissed Dad, still shovelling. 'All right. Go on.' I could hear him trying to push the bag into the cupboard under the sink as I opened the door.

It was Terry from IT. 'Is your dad in?' he said.

I took him through to the living room. 'I heard about your intruder and wondered if there was anything we could do as a Homewatch group by way of support.'

'It's a bit late for that, Terry,' said Dad.

'We can access back-up from Victim Support, help you deal with the insurance company forms and all that. Or if you need short-term financial assistance . . .'

Dorothy sort of hiccuped a laugh at this. Terry stared at her. 'Pot of tea?' she offered.

'No. Thanks. They made a right mess of your tree. What's the point of that? It's just plain envy, isn't it? They can't stand it that you've worked hard and reaped the rewards. They think if they want something they can just take it. Because they haven't got it in them to really earn this stuff. That's what it is. If you ask me.'

'Dead right,' said Dad. He had his hands behind his back.

'Oh. Missed something anyway,' said Terry, and he bent down and picked up a pair of twenty-pound notes from near Dad's feet. He held them out to Dad. Dad hesitated.

'Oh. Sure they're not yours?' Dad said.

'Well, they were on your carpet,' said Terry, a bit surprised.

I realized that Dad still had a fistful of money. He couldn't put his hand out to take them. He said, 'Just, errrm, put them down . . . in case of fingerprints.' You could see where Anthony got it from.

'Oh, God, yeah,' gasped Terry. 'I never thought of that.' And he dropped the notes like they were red-hot. They fluttered back to the floor.

'I like your tie,' said Dorothy.

'Yeah. I like it too,' said Dad, too quickly. Then he sat down suddenly on the big chair with his hands still behind him. I could see that he was trying to stuff his fistful of twenties down behind the cushion.

That's when I decided to go to bed. When I saw that the money had made Dad scared of Terry from IT.

I got a fright when I went into my room. There was someone sitting on the end of my bed. It was Anthony. He held up his hand and said, 'I'm listening.'

I listened too. I could hear Terry's tie playing the *Scooby-Doo* theme. Then I heard him saying goodbye and the front door closing after him. Then I heard . . .

'Shush,' said Anthony. 'Now. What can you hear?'

'Counting.' They were counting the money.

'She's got him counting it. Can you believe that? Talk about rubbing it in. She is pure evil.'

'How do you mean?'

'Oh, come on, we come home and find the house turned over and there she is on the doorstep. What a coincidence!'

'You think she did the burglary?'

'She was looking for the money. If only she'd known what an utter sucker Dad is. She must've been pretty surprised and pleased when he just told her all about it.'

Downstairs Dad suddenly burst out laughing. A big, happy laugh, as though someone was tickling him.

'She'll wait till his back is turned and run off with the lot.' Anthony went back to his own room.

I lay there on the bed listening to the voices downstairs – counting and laughing, then start-ing to count again. After a while, I was aware that the talking had stopped. I wondered how long for. When I looked around, I realized Dad was standing behind the half-open door, watching me.

'What?'

'Why aren't you asleep? D'you want a story?'

'Dad . . . the money . . .'

'Is owed me.'

'What?'

'I work every minute God sends just to cover the mortgage to give you a decent home. I am drowning in debt. I'm permanently knackered. And now everything I've worked for is wrecked. I've had enough now. This is it. This is payback time. We're going to town tomorrow to change it and then we're going to spend it. Now goodnight.'

After he'd gone I got out of bed and tried to sleep on the floor. I thought I could hear something moving up above me, on the other side of the ceiling. Someone was on the roof or maybe inside the roof.

I went out on to the landing and stood outside Dad's bedroom door. I wasn't sure whether to wake him, in case it was someone only I could hear. The sound followed me. It was right over my head now. Something touched my hair. I looked up. Nothing there. Just the hatch to the loft. Then a fine shower of dust fell down and landed in my eye. The hatch was moving. Suddenly it disappeared and I was looking up into a window of darkness.

Cold air poured down on me. Then it was like one clot of darkness had come away from the rest and was dripping down through the hatch – two long dangly gobs of dark were dangling right over my head. They seemed to be both attached to some bigger dark at the top. They dropped on to the floor and it was only then that I saw they were legs and it was a body with a face that was looking right into mine. The man with the glass eye had jumped down from the loft and was crouching in front of me. He put his finger on his lips. I didn't scream. I had the feeling it wouldn't be the right thing to do.

'In there,' he said, pointing to my room. When he talked he barely opened his mouth. It was like he was talking inside my head. It was like listening to fear.

I went back into my room and sat on the bed. He came in, closed the door and looked around. 'I know you've got it. It's mine,' he said. 'You're going to change it tomorrow and that's a good thing. Saves me a job. Understand?'

I nodded. I was trying to look him in the eye so that he'd know I was telling the truth, but then I thought perhaps I was looking in his glass eye, so I looked in the other one. He picked up the mobile phone from the bedside table and started to poke at it, looking for the number. I tried to make conversation. I said, 'Was it you who burgled us, then?'

'What? Nothing's been stolen, has it? I just want what's mine. I couldn't find it. So I thought I'd wait for you.'

So the burglary wasn't really a burglary, just like the train robbery wasn't really a train robbery. Both times it was just a way of hiding someone. Glass Eye crouched down in front of me and breathed words into my face. 'This is what you're going to do for me. Tomorrow night, when you've done the job and everyone else is in bed, I'm going to call you on this phone. You're going to come down, open the front door and let me in. Then I'm going to take the money and go. OK? I won't say a word. And you won't have to worry about it any more.'

To be logical about it, I actually had something in common with Glass Eye: we were the only ones who knew the money was a worry. When he said that about worrying, I knew he understood the money better than Dad or Anthony or any of the others.

'Just keep your phone switched on,' he said. Then he was gone.

I sat on my bed for a while, just to be on the safe side. Then I decided I didn't want to be in my room any more. I went out on to the landing. I didn't really want to stand under the hatch to the loft again, so that put Dad's room out of reach. I went down to the kitchen. The donkey saddlebags were lying on the table with a mostly drunk bottle of wine, two glasses and a plate of crusts. Dad and Dorothy must've made toast while they were counting. I put my head on the saddlebags and listened to the comfortable tummy-rumbling of the central heating.

I must've fallen asleep because I didn't hear her come in. I just felt the tug at the saddlebags. I sat up and Dorothy was standing there, looking down at me.

'Hi,' I said.

She put her finger to her lips and went, 'Shush.'

Dorothy put the saddlebags over her shoulder, opened the back door quietly and slipped out.

I didn't say anything. I didn't move until the door clicked back into place. Then I ran to the front window and ducked under the curtains to look out. She was putting the money on the back seat of the car. The yellow internal lights were on so I could see her clearly behind the glass as she put the key in the ignition. She looked across to the house. The internal lights went off as the engine started up but she was still looking at me. She did her unique little finger-only wave. Then the red indicator light started to pulse and she drove away. Her car was a Smarties-yellow Vauxhall Nova. '*No va*' is Spanish for 'don't go' or 'doesn't go'. But this one went. Obviously a mistake in the translation.

17

The patron saint of motorists is St Christopher (no dates, probably legendary), obviously. The story they always tell about him is that he was this huge great bouncer who decided to work for the king of some country which I don't know. Then he discovered that the king was scared of Death, so he thought, well, I'm not working for second best, I'll go and work for Death. So he goes off to work for Death – I don't know what he did exactly; you wouldn't think Death would need much help. Anyway, it turns out that Death is scared of something too – namely the child Jesus, so Christopher . . . well, you can see where this is headed. It turns out that the whole thing is utterly and completely fictional, obviously. In fact, rubbish. So there never was a St Christopher and he's officially banned, along with St Pyr, who was found dead drunk at the bottom of a well and made into a saint by clerical error.

So motorists are like liars and estate agents. They don't have a patron saint. When Dorothy picked up our money and drove away, no one was looking after her. And that was the thing which kept happening with the money. People helped themselves and then no one could help them.

I was still behind the curtain when Dad came down. I was staring at the road, in case she did come back. I heard him panicking with Anthony.

'The money's gone. And she was here and now she's gone too. Her car's not there.'

'And neither is our Damian,' said Anthony.

'No,' I shouted. 'I'm here. I'm behind the curtain.'

Dad pulled the curtain back. He said, 'Where's Dorothy?'

'I don't know. She came in, took the money and went. I don't even know how she got in.'

'She took the money? All of it?'

Anthony shrugged. 'I did say. I did warn you.'

'Just be quiet. Damian, come on, think. What did she say?'

'She said, "Shush."'

'And what did you say?'

'I shushed.'

Dad groaned and threw himself into the big chair. Then he sat up straight, remembering something. He rooted down the back of the chair and came out with the fistful of twenties he'd hidden last night. He was surprised and disappointed to discover that there wasn't that much. 'A hundred and twenty. A hundred and twenty quid out of . . . how much?'

Anthony said, 'Two hundred and twenty-nine thousand, three—'

'OK, thank you, Anthony. Thank you and be quiet.'

'I did say.'

'Not only did you say, you also said that you said and now you're saying that you said that you said, so that's enough saying, all right?' Dad lowered his voice and started talking to himself instead of us. 'Think what to do,' he said 'Think what to do.' Suddenly he ran off upstairs and came down with his mobile. He found her number in incoming calls, gave a happy yelp and dialled it.

Anthony put on a robot voice and droned, 'The vodaphone you are calling is switched off . . .'

It was as well.

Dad glared at him. 'The charity. The charity she was working for. What was it called?'

'Water Aid.'

He got their number from Directory Enquiries. 'You two wait in there,' he said, pointing to the living room. He carried on talking to the phone. 'Oh. I see. The collections are done by a franchise.' Water Aid didn't know anything about Dorothy. 'What's the name of the franchise? Thank you.'

He dialled another number and looked up at us. 'Nearly there,' he said. 'I'm in a queue.' He sat on the bottom of the stairs. We could just about hear a tinny orchestra playing down the line. He sat there, saying nothing, listening to the music. He kept the mobile clamped to his ear and tried Dorothy again on the landline.

'She knows it's you,' said Anthony. 'She won't answer if she knows it's you. If you press 141 before you dial her number, it withholds your number so she won't know it's you.'

'How do you know that? Why would you need to know that?'

'Just try it and see. If she doesn't know it's you . . .'

'I thought I told you to be quiet. Get the fairy lights picked up and put them back in the box.'

'Are we not putting the tree back up again?'

'No, we're not. Go on. Get cracking.'

Anthony started to untangle the fairy lights from the wreck of the tree. Dad put down his mobile and said, 'What was that number again?'

'141.'

He dialled. Then he redialled. Redialled again. Thirteen redials. Then he sat down on the big chair, checking behind the cushion one more time just in case. Nothing. We all sat and listened to the clock nibbling away at the last few hours of sterling.

I persuaded Anthony to have a game of Top Trumps. We didn't dare go upstairs for his 'Predators' set, so we tried playing with my saint cards. On the 'Predators' set you score points for ferocity and weight of the predators. We used saints' dates and feast days instead. It was rubbish. I won in about thirty seconds because I knew them all. Anthony doesn't even know his own saint's day.

I looked at the telly, even though it wasn't

switched on. I could see the Digibox and the wires leading out to the aerial up on the roof, where signals bombarded it from the masts and transmitters on their lonely hilltops being blasted with other signals from satellites which were drifting around in space catching the signals from earth and bouncing them back down again – television signals and phone signals, and signals for ships and cars – so that the whole air was like a cat's cradle of beams and waves and rays and messages.

I was holding my St Clare card at the time and I thought about how she used to send a vision of herself through the air when she was in her hermitage. There were no phones or tellies then, so the air was completely empty apart from birds and this vision of St Clare. I wondered if it could still be done.

I could see my face reflected on the dead screen of the telly. I tried to imagine it being sucked back into the cable, up through the wire and spat out of the aerial. I could see it shooting through the air, past the tangles of phone chat and radio stations, floating off into space. I tried to see the flocks of wandering satellites up there and St Clare shepherding them around in her capacity as patron saint of broadcast media. The satellites looked a bit like floating monstrances. I imagined banging into one and then bouncing back towards earth, picking up speed, blazing like a comet through re-entry, whistling through the jet stream, punching through the cloud cover, until there underneath me was a mess of wires and circuits with something shining in the middle. The wires and circuits were a town and the shining thing was the glass roof of its station. I passed through the roof like a beam of light and stood on the platform while people rushed by me to get on the train. People were kissing each other goodbye. People were checking their watches. People were carefully carrying paper cups of coffee.

Dorothy walked past me and into the carriage.

I saw her through the window, chatting to a lady at her table and settling down. I stepped back. For some reason I was scared that she might see me. She picked up a big bag and tried to swing it on to the luggage rack. It was heavy – probably full of money. She must have missed, because the bag came down again and thudded on to the table. She smiled a sorry at the lady and looked out of the window. She saw me. There was no doubt about it. It was like being punched. I thought I was invisible. In fact I thought I was dreaming. But she could see me. Even though I was still at home. I was sending her a vision of me.

Suddenly I could see Dad again and Anthony and the living room. They were in between me and her, like when you look out of a window in the dark and you can see what's in front of you through the glass and what's behind you on the glass. Dad and Anthony and me were on the glass. Through the glass was the train and Dorothy looking at me. I heard a whistle blow. There was a bit of fuss. I saw her wrinkle her eyebrows as if she was trying to figure out what I was doing there. I heard the engines fire up. I stepped back and I was still in the living room, where no one was talking.

Dad looked over at me, as though he'd heard me come into the room, even though I'd never left it. He still didn't say anything. He looked over at the window. Then he frowned. Then he leaned forward and frowned some more. Then he stood up. I looked where he was looking. Dorothy was striding up towards the front door, waving through the window. Dad pulled the front door open like it was a Christmas cracker. There was a huge red people carrier – a Toyota Previa – outside.

'Did you think I'd run off and left you?'

'No,' said Dad.

'Yes,' said Anthony.

'Anthony did,' said Dad.

'I was just a bit eager. And thorough, you know.'

'Eager and thorough, just what I said,' said Dad. He was bouncing up and down on the soles of his feet.

'I went into work. I bought the car for cash. It seemed like a good way of getting rid of a stack. Buy it now in sterling. Sell it next week in euros. We'll lose a bit but not much. They hold their value, these. Oh, and I changed 2,000 in the bank. We've still got 150,000 and one afternoon to change it all. Can we change it?'

Dad yelled, 'Yes, we can!'

Ten minutes later we were in the back of the Previa driving towards Manchester, because they've got more banks there. The word 'Previa', by the way, doesn't mean anything at all. When they discovered that you couldn't sell a car called 'Nova' in Spain, they started hiring people to think up names for cars that would be completely meaningless in every country on earth. That way they would know that the car's name didn't mean 'Uncomfortable' in Serbian or 'Dangerous' in Welsh. So there are these people who sit around trying to think up words that mean nothing at all. Imagine that. Previa is one of those words, and so is Megane and so is . . . Well, there's loads of them. If you just think of all the people on motorways driving round with no patron saint and words that don't mean anything written all over their cars, lexically speaking, it's a worry.

Anthony said, 'If the banks are busy, we could try the bureau de change. We don't have to change the money into euros, we could change it into dollars. In fact, we might be better off. There'll be a rush on the euro this week because of us joining, so its value will go right up. If we go for dollars and wait for the situation to calm down, we'll probably come out ahead. What d'you think?'

Dad said, 'I think I brought the wrong child home from the hospital. Where did I get you, Anthony?'

When we got to Manchester, Dorothy suggested that we split up. She'd take me to all the banks on the north side of Deansgate and Dad would take Anthony to all the ones on the south, 'Just in case we have to queue.'

Deansgate was quiet as we hurried past the giant Christmas tree. It was quiet because everyone was already in the bank. Opening the door was like accidentally joining an attempt to break the world record for fitting as many people as possible in one place. From somewhere very far away, we could hear a robot voice saying, 'Window 3 is free. Please go to Window 3.' Sometimes it would say, 'To change smaller amounts, please use the machine on the left of the hall,' but nobody ever did.

Dorothy got twitchy. She tried to push me into the next queue in case it went faster, but when I ducked under the rope, a man in a duffel coat pushed me back.

Dorothy fiddled with her bag. I kept a lookout while she slid a few more thousand out of the bag and into her pocket. When I glanced down to see if she'd finished, I saw her train ticket in the open bag. She turned round to smile at me but I turned away just in time.

We finally got to the till. The face of the woman behind the glass was red and sweaty, as though it was a summer's day. She kept talking to the man at the next window. We couldn't hear what they were saying because of the glass. Dorothy slid her wads of notes under the window. The woman picked them up and tidied them. She said, 'How much is here, please?'

'Five thousand.'

'It's a bit much. Are you an account holder?'

'No. I was going to buy a car today but it's not ready. I've been saving for three months to buy it and now it's not ready, so I've got to change this . . .'

'It's an unusually large amount.'

'Well, that's why I don't want to lose it, love.'

The woman was looking around. She was going to call a supervisor.

'It's not an unusually large amount to spend on a car, I can tell you.'

The supervisor was busy. The red-faced woman went a shade redder. I started to bounce up and down on my heels. I tugged at Dorothy's sleeve. She snapped at me, 'What? What do you want?'

'I need a wee.'

'Oh, brilliant. We queue for half an hour, finally get to the window and now you need a wee.'

'I can't help it.'

The red-faced woman had her back to us now, waving at her supervisor. Dorothy knocked on the glass and pointed to me. I was up and down like a yo-yo now. 'Have you got a toilet? A customer toilet?'

'I'm afraid not.'

'Well, you must have something. Where do you go?'

'I go on this side. It's secure, this side. You can't come through without clearance. There's toilets in Marks & Spencer's, just up the road.'

'So am I supposed to go to Marks & Spencer's, come back and go to the back of the queue with my hard-earned savings and just hope that I get to the front of the queue before you close? I need this car for work. If I don't change this money I've had it. I can't . . .'

'All right. All right.' She stacked the money in a counting machine and gave Dorothy 7,042 euros in a long brown envelope.

Dorothy was flustered and edgy. She almost dragged me along the street. 'Right,' she said, 'M & S, where's M & S?'

I said, 'I don't really need a wee.' It took her a minute to understand. 'I just thought it would put a bit of pressure on her, you know.'

'Well, you little belter,' she whooped. I took that as a compliment. 'You 100 per cent blinder.' I took that as a compliment too. 'You cunning little crook.' I wasn't so happy with that.

We ran to Barclays. It worked there as well. And in the Halifax, HSBC, the Royal Bank of Scotland and in Lloyds. The only place it didn't work was the Co-op, because they had a customer toilet. By four o'clock we'd changed 62,000 pounds. The banks were starting to close.

'There's got to be somewhere else.'

'There's a bank inside Kendal's.' As soon as I said it, I wished I hadn't. She took hold of my hand and nearly dragged me back up Deansgate and in through the main door. The main door leads in to the make-up department, where Mum used to work.

The last time I came here . . . Well, it doesn't matter. She worked on the Clinique counter, that's all you need to know. It's over by the lifts.

I used to like it that when we came to collect her, we could see her before she saw us. You could watch her chatting to a customer, or to the other woman on the counter, or tidying up, and she wouldn't know you were looking at her. She wore a white overall with a black name badge on it. All the women who worked there had skin like hers – skin that was shinier and smoother than everyone else's. And they were all so clean, immaculate really. There was always beautiful music playing. There was now. And all the immaculate women were still here. Except for her.

One of the immaculate women – the one from the Chanel counter – stared at me, as if she was going to say something. Which was bad. Then she looked as though she couldn't think what to say. Which was worse.

I decided to get out quickly. I said, 'The bank's upstairs,' but when I turned round, I saw my own reflection in a big mirror. No sign of Dorothy. I looked around and saw the Chanel woman looking at me again. Only now I could see that her skin wasn't smooth. It had some kind of paste over it to make it look smooth. She'd missed a bit round her ear. It looked silly. I wondered if Mum had ever done that. I looked behind me. No Dorothy. Just a big cutout of a thin brown sweaty woman in a bikini. To be medical about it, my breathing was irregular.

Someone touched me on the shoulder and I swung around. Dorothy. I had to swallow to stop myself crying.

She looked around, then looked at me. 'How do you know about the bank?'

I still couldn't catch my breath.

'Is this is where your mum used to work?'

She didn't wait for me to answer. She just said, 'I've had enough of queuing up now, let's go and have a bit of a spree.'

I didn't actually want any worldly goods, but I thought it might be rude to say so. I followed her up the escalator. She was rooting in her bag. At the top she took something out and dropped it in the bin. I saw that it was the train ticket.

Dorothy didn't take me to the toy department or the electrical goods. She took me to boyswear, picked out a bright-red duffel coat and held it up against me. It had a hood that pulled right up over your head so it looked like a Franciscan habit. She said, 'Paddington Bear!' which was another way of putting it. As far as worldly goods go, it was the best I've seen in ages.

It was probably the only thing in the shop that I really liked. She bought it for me. 'I bet he hasn't bought you a coat in ages. Coats and cutlery, they're the things that dads never buy.'

She bought herself a bag.

On the way back up King Street we saw an amusement arcade that had a sign up saying 'Still Accepting Sterling Silver'. It was fantastic! I've never been in one before. There's a thing where you drop coins on to a kind of tray that goes backwards and forwards and the idea is to get your coin to tip all the others off. I won twice!

'Just what we needed,' said Dorothy, 'another bag of old money.'

You could spend it in there. We bought a fantastic

Egyptian vase and some candyfloss, the kind that comes in a bag.

We met Dad and Anthony back at the car. Dad said, 'Did you change it all?'

'We lost interest, didn't we, Damian? Want some candyfloss?' Dad tugged a big wad out of the bag. 'How much did you get?'

'Well,' said Dad, 'we had this brilliant idea that we'd take the money to the building society and pay off the house.'

'Fantastic. Were they OK about it?'

'They were shut.'

'Oh.'

'We got seventy grand.'

'We got sixty-two. Sorry.'

'So we'll just have to make do with 132,000 grand.'

'And a new Previa.'

'And a Gamecube Flight Simulator. Plasma-screen TV. And dishwasher, which was Anthony's idea.'

'Oh, well, then.'

The car was crammed with stuff.

They were really happy. Even Anthony was happy. I think I was even happy too for a minute.

Then my phone buzzed. It was a text message. It wasn't from him. It was from Anthony, saying, 'We R W8ing', over a picture of Dad by the new car. He must have sent it a few minutes before. It was nothing to worry about, but it reminded me that I had plenty to worry about.

Guardian angels are supposed to look after you, but they know when you're going to die, obviously. It must make them sad, watching you playing footie or having your tea or whatever and knowing exactly when it will all end. That's how I felt that evening. The others were that happy. They bought an Indian takeaway and ate it round the coffee table, with the bags of new money on the floor, and they talked about what they were going to do with it all.

Dad was still big on holidays. He made a list of faraway names – Acapulco, Bondi, Barcelona – and Dorothy came back with her own – Capri, Sardinia and Greenland for the Northern Lights.

Anthony was still on about real estate. He'd seen an advert for barn conversions in the Lleyn Peninsula. 'You could rent it out – so it would be generating a stream of income while at the same time increasing its capital value.'

'They must be very small barns,' said Dad.

'Why?'

'Lleyn Peninsula, it's all sheep, isn't it? No cows. You'd have to rent it out to midgets.'

'Or sheep.'

They were so happy, they were just looking for an excuse to laugh. Sheep kept them laughing for about five hours. I tried to join in, but I was just thinking, one more sheep joke and then it'll all be gone. It was eight o'clock.

Sometimes something starts as a joke but no one wants it to stop so it just keeps going until it turns real. I don't know whose idea it was, but half an hour later Dad was mixing a bucket of wallpaper paste. They were going to paper Anthony's room with the rest of the old money.

Anthony was spreading newspaper out on his carpet. Dorothy put the trestle table up on the landing and started singing 'Money, Money, Money'. She and Dad started slopping all the old tens and twenties with glue and Anthony placed them carefully on his wall, smoothing out each one with a brush and making sure they were all nicely lined up, as though they were bathroom tiles. They were covering up the footballer wallpaper with old banknotes.

Dorothy was the most out of control. She kept saying, 'I can't believe I'm doing this', and in between she'd tell jokes. 'I saw three Barbies waiting for the toilet and I thought, hello, it's a Barbie-queue. Barbecue. Get it?' She didn't wait to find out if we did or not. 'What d'you call a deer with no eyes? No–eye-dear. No idea! What do you call a deer with no eyes and no legs? Still-no-eye-dear. Still no idea!'

Then I noticed something strange. I was laughing too. I didn't care any more about Glass Eye. What did it matter about the money? Dad had a new car. He'd had a great day. He had a new friend. He was laughing. My dad was laughing. I got so I was worried that she'd run out of jokes and it would all be over. So I went and got my copy of *The Ha Ha Bonk Book* – which has thousands of jokes in it – and every time she couldn't think of one, I'd read one out. And when I read one out, that would remind her of another one. And it went on until we all sounded like penguins on laughing gas.

'What d'you call a man with a spade in his head?'

'Doug. Dug!'

The jokes were actually funnier when everyone knew the punchline, because then we could all shout out together.

'What do you call a donkey with three legs?'

'A wonky!'

And all the time the wall was more and more covered with portraits of the Queen or Florence Nightingale or Charles Dickens or whoever, and the glue was getting everywhere.

'What do you call a donkey with a drinking problem?'

'A plonky!'

I noticed that Anthony didn't join in on this one. Maybe he just didn't know the punchline.

'A panda goes into a pub and orders a sandwich . . .' said Dorothy.

She wasn't looking at anyone. She was concentrating on the wallpapering. She didn't notice Anthony slip out of the room.

'Panda eats the sandwich, shoots the barman and goes. The police catch him and say, What did you do that for?'

Anthony would have gone to his room except we were all in there redecorating it.

'Panda says . . . I'm a panda; that's what I do. Look me up in the dictionary. So they do and it says,

"Panda bear, from China, eats shoots and leaves."
See? Eats, shoots and leaves.'

'Very good,' said Dad.

But he didn't laugh. He was fixated on the wall-paper now and so was she. They could've stopped any time but they were hypnotized. It wasn't a laugh any more. It was a job. They wouldn't stop until every old note was on the wall. I could just see a footballer's head sticking out above the twenty I was pasting up, and I suddenly remembered how much Anthony had loved his footballer wallpaper. I sneaked out after him.

Anthony was in my room, squatting on the end of the bed, like Glass Eye, only angrier.

'This is all your fault,' he hissed.

'I know.'

'You don't know. You don't know what you've done.'

In the next room, Dad suddenly burst out laughing at one of her jokes.

'Hear that? He'll be laughing on the other side of his face when she goes and leaves him, won't he? Remember what he was like when Mum went?'

'Maybe she won't go? You said she was going to go yesterday but she came back. Maybe she . . .'

229

'Is that what you want? Her here instead of Mum? Her in this house? With her stupid jokes and lasagne with no sweetcorn. Do you want her here instead of Mum?'

I hadn't thought of that.

'You did it all. It's all down to you. You and your weird stuff. Chucking money away, talking to yourself, seeing things. You are not normal. You are a problem.'

'Don't say that.'

'Wherever she is, you're not going there, because you are a nutter. You're a nutter and you should be locked up.'

18

There's a lot of confusion about angels. Like when we were in the best place and the nurses were supposed to be angels. Or in the graveyard, there were stones that said 'Little Angel' or 'Now with the Angels'. People are not angels. And when you die, you do not become an angel. Angels are a completely different species. For instance, they've got no bellybuttons, obviously, as they weren't born. You'd need totally different bone structure and DNA and everything if you wanted to be an angel. So no one becomes an angel to watch over you. Ever. No one. It's a biological impossibility.

Also, there are different kinds of angel – e.g.

cherubim, seraphim, powers and dominions – and some of them are HUGE. Like your guardian angel is about six metres high. It's embarrassing when you think about it that you need all that celestial power and wingspan just to keep you out of trouble. And it doesn't even work a lot of the time.

I lay in my bed, looking up at the ceiling, wishing it would open up and suck me into the pitch black and leave me behind the water tank. I had the mobile in my hand, set to vibrate so it wouldn't wake the others.

My phone shook. I held it up over my head. Glass Eye was looking down at me from the video screen. He whispered, 'Ten minutes,' and flashed the fingers of one hand at me twice. I nodded and went down to get the money.

As I passed the front door, I could hear voices outside. It must be him. He must have someone with him. It sounded like more than a few. Maybe he'd brought the whole gang. I could hear one of them saying, 'Ring the doorbell.' I was scared they'd wake Dad. I was scared full stop.

I opened the door. It wasn't Glass Eye.

It was a man with three little girls. Before I'd

even asked him who he was, he'd started, 'See these little girls, my girls, these are the girls that Santa Claus forgot. D'you see what I'm saying?'

I didn't. I looked over his shoulder to see if Glass Eye was coming, but it was too dark.

'You're our last hope. We haven't even got the bus fare home because there's no point going back if you don't help us. The landlord'll chuck us out. Come on, we don't want much. If you could see us through . . .'

He was pushing the girls towards me and I saw now that one of them was Gemma. She whispered, 'Sorry about this. Tricia Springer told us you gave her three grand for carol-singing. We are on the bones of our, you know. Don't tell anyone.'

'What do you want? I mean, how much?'

'Oh, thanks a lot, son,' said her dad. 'A couple of hundred. Maybe three would get us through . . .'

The bag was behind the door. I grabbed a handful of notes from the top and handed it over, thinking, I wonder if Tricia told anyone else.

The man said, 'Yes!' and punched the air as he led the girls away. When they stepped back out from the door, they triggered the reactive halogen light. And then I saw it.

The whole close was packed with people.

Hundreds of people all pushing and shouldering their way down the path towards the door. Each and every eye was staring at me. Each and every eye was full of want or need. There were hundreds. It felt like millions.

I remembered what St Peter had said about putting our address on the back of the envelopes. He'd been right. Well, he was infallible. We were besieged. Hoping it was a dream, I shut the door too quickly. It woke Dad. From upstairs, he shouted sleepily, 'Damian, who are you talking to?'

'No one. Just checking.'

Then the doorbell rang. I froze. It was him. It must be Glass Eye. I had to answer. The others were just a dream. While I was thinking, Dad was coming downstairs, muttering, 'Who is it at this time of night.'

'I'll get it.'

'Don't be daft.' He yanked the door open and a woman in a smart suit stepped right in, saying, 'Some 50 per cent of families with a chronically ill child break up. Long-term care is stressful and impoverishing. We aim to give people a break and to help them over the hardest times with simple things like train fares and overnight expenses for as little as . . .'

'What the . . . Do you know what time it is? This is a private house. There's kids.'

'Exactly. Kids. Kids are what it's all about. Kids with chronic illness, as if that wasn't hard enough to deal with in itself, but all too often that illness leads to the break-up of the child's family.'

'Look, it sounds great, but come back in the morning, eh?'

Dad was trying to push her back out, but the minute he did, a tall man with sticky-up hair was standing in his way, holding up something like a tiny ladder. 'This may look like a tiny ladder to you, but to a hedgehog it's a lifeline. It's the difference between life and death.' It was a little ladder actually. It was for helping hedgehogs out of cattle grids and drains. 'They cost eight pounds a time to manufacture and install. With your help we could save hundreds of hedgehogs.'

'Why me?'

'Oh, come on, everyone knows. Why not give us a handful? This delightful ceramic hedgehog will be yours to keep.'

'In the morning. We'll talk in the morning. Now, come on. Please. There's kids . . .' and he pointed at me.

But it was no good. Everyone just started

shouting and waving leaflets and pictures. The reactive halogen light snapped on and off like lightning. It felt like the whole population of the world was trying to get through our front door.

'Look, this is that same donkey after only three months in our care!'

'You may be asking yourself, why does Waterloo Station need friends?'

'I know that irritable bowel syndrome isn't sexy . . .'

'. . . and if you gift-aid your donation, then it's worth 30 per cent more to us without costing you a penny. I've got the forms here.'

'Yoga for prisoners . . .'

While Dad was shouting at them, I quietly picked up the bag of cash and took down my new red duffel coat. I slipped into the living room. There was someone banging on the window. He was pressing a photograph of a woman in a headscarf up against the glass, yelling, 'They want to send her back tomorrow. They say I can appeal, but how to appeal with no money? She have no one back home. They all dead.'

He hadn't finished when someone shoved him out of the way and started knocking on the glass too. It felt like the whole house was about to crumple under the weight of people's needs. They all looked angry and desperate. Dad was shouting, 'Anthony, shut the door,' as though he thought that they were going to just burst in and take the money. I could see he was scared, just like he'd been scared of Terry from IT. I made my decision.

I opened the back door. There was no one there. At the bottom of the garden, I dropped the bag over the fence and climbed over after it. I could still hear them shouting. I could hear them all the way to the railway line. When I got to the holly bushes, the phone buzzed. Glass Eye was growling at me through the video screen. 'Where the hell are you? What the hell is going on?' I dropped the phone. He carried on yelling into it. The screen glittered as I walked away, like a talking raindrop. Looking back towards Cromarty Close, I could see a pale blue light flashing on and off and I knew the police had arrived.

It was Anthony who told me what happened later. Lots of police had come because the neighbours had complained about the noise. The police got everyone out of the house and then Dad had to try to explain to them why all these people thought he had a load of money. Dad just said, 'I don't know. Someone must've been saying things about us.'

'Untrue things, obviously.'

'Obviously.'

But the community policeman was there by then. He picked out the new plasma-screen TV and the dishwasher right away and said, 'So has the Good Lord been pouring out his comforts and consolations on you and all, then?'

Dad said, 'What?'

'Mind if I take a look round?' said the copper. And off he went upstairs.

Dad hissed at Anthony, 'Where is it? Where is it all?' because he couldn't see the bag of money anywhere. It was Anthony who noticed that my coat was missing as well. He didn't say anything. He knew where I'd be. He sneaked the back door open. And there, on the patio, was Glass Eye.

He leaned down right into Anthony's face and hissed, 'You're the clever one, aren't you? You were clever with me last time. Don't try to be clever with me this time or I'll drown you. OK?'

Anthony stood back to let him in.

'Where is it?'

Anthony said it was upstairs. Glass Eye pushed him forward. Anthony led him up to his bedroom.

And the first thing Glass Eye saw, before he was inside the room even, was the wall completely covered with old money. They don't take the glue very well by the way, so they'd started to bubble a bit. It looked like the money was crawling up the walls. Glass Eye walked in there and stared at it up close, like he couldn't believe it. He touched it. It was only then he realized the community policeman was in the room already. 'Did you know,' said the policeman, 'that 70 per cent of British banknotes contain traces of cocaine? Some 40-odd per cent contain traces of gunpowder. You know, from guns. It's all on there. If you could read it. That's the thing, isn't it, you can't read it. Them notes. People have sweated for them, stolen them, wasted them, died longing for them, and what do the notes care? Not a thing. Now. Who are you?'

Glass Eye put his head on one side to look at the man with his good eye. 'Who am I? Who the hell are you?' he said.

'We're the police,' said the community policeman.

19

I was next to the track by then. The up-train went screaming past in a mighty rushing wind of diesel and noise. It blew away the sound of the shouting from the Close and tossed my hair around. Even the big fat white moon seemed to shake as it went by. When it had gone, I had thirteen minutes till the next train came. I stepped on to the track. The rails were shining blue. They looked like a long metal ladder leading all the way to the moon and the moon looked like the entrance to a tunnel full of light.

I tipped the bag of money out on to the track. I had taken a box of matches from the kitchen. I tried to light one. It blew out before it lit properly. I put a ten-euro note between my teeth and lit that from the next match. It burned really quickly. I dropped it on to the pile. I thought it was going to blow out right away, but another note caught fire first and then another and then another, and soon dozens of them were blazing. As they burned they rose into the air, carried up by their own heat. Soon they were dancing all around me, like a confetti of fire. I started to laugh and out of nowhere a charm of zebra finches flew through the middle of them, twittering madly. The gust of their wings seemed to make the fire brighter and more and more sheets of flame whooshed into the air. I put my arms out and spun around, whirling the flames higher and higher.

When I stopped, that's when I saw her. She was sitting down, which surprised me. She obviously had been there a while, watching me.

I said, 'I know you're only a dream, but I don't care. It's nice to see you, even in a dream.'

She smiled. Then she looked past me at the fire. Its rosy glow spread over her cheek. Her skin was shiny and perfect. She wasn't wearing foundation or a tinted moisturizer. She just had better skin than other mothers.

I said, 'I tried to be good with it, but the money just makes everything worse.'

She stood up and for a minute I thought she was going to walk away. I shouted, 'Talk to me,' and then more quietly, 'please.'

She looked at her watch. She said, 'Two minutes, OK? And listen. I am your mother after all and I'm dead, so I know what I'm talking about. All right?'

Of course it was all right.

'You need to use conditioner on your hair. Your dad won't think of that, but it makes all the difference. Believe me. Dental hygiene. It's no good saying your prayers and then forgetting to brush your teeth. If you get a gum infection, it'll colour your outlook and you'll lose your zest. You can't move in purgatory for people with no zest and it's all so avoidable. Now, Anthony. He seems to have taken it better than you but he hasn't. He's got a good heart. He just, well, he doesn't know where it is. He's going to need you. Be good to him. Me. You are not to worry about me. You have been worrying about me, haven't you?'

I just nodded.

'Well, don't. It's very interesting where I am. We're kept very busy.'

'What about Dad?'

'Well, obviously you should be good to him as well. He is your father.'

'No, but I mean, couldn't you talk to him?'

'What about?'

I wasn't sure whether to say.

'He can't see me anyway.'

'Why not?' I knew why not really. I looked back towards the house.

'It's her, isn't it? Your dad and her. Damian, you know how complicated the money was? Well, people are even more complicated. You want things to be good or bad. But things are complicated. The thing to remember is that there's nearly always enough good around to be going on with. You've just got to have a bit of faith, you know. And if you've got faith in people, that makes them stronger. And you . . . you've got enough to sort all three of you out. That's why I'm counting on you.'

I said, 'I've not been worrying about you. I've been missing you.'

She said, 'Well, that's allowed.'

Then I asked her. 'Anthony says you're not a saint.'

'Well, the criteria are very strict. It's not just a

case of being very good and all that. You do have to do an actual miracle.'

'So . . .'

'Oh, I'm in there. Course I am.'

'What was your miracle?'

'Don't you know?' She looked me up and down, then said very quietly, 'It was you.'

In the distance I could hear Anthony calling me. She looked at her watch. 'One oh four. Step off the track, then.'

The up-train was coming. I stepped off the track backwards and so did she. So we were on opposite sides of the track. The train rushed between us. I was sure she wouldn't be there when all the carriages had gone. But she was. She was still there. I grinned.

Anthony was nearer and louder now. I yelled, 'Coming!' and turned to go to him.

She said, 'Hey.'

I looked back at her.

'Aren't you going to say goodbye?'

I ran across the line and hugged her. She smelt of Clinique Everyday and rain. She was warm. At least I think she was warm. It could have been the heat from the burning money, gusting towards me. Then I felt her wedding ring snag in my hair.

And I knew it was a real hug. It made all the things that had kept her from me seem like dreams. She whispered, 'Be good to him.' Then she was gone.

'What have you done?' It was Anthony.

He knew what I'd done really. I didn't say anything. I just started to walk back to the house. He followed me. I wasn't looking at him when I said, 'Did you see her?'

He didn't say no. He said, 'What did she say?'

I stopped and turned to face him. 'She was pleased with us. She says we're going to be all right.'

We set off for the house.

'Damian,' Anthony said, 'you're not a nutter by the way.'

'I know,' I said, 'but you are.' I laughed and ran off.

'Right. You've had it.' He chased after me. We were doing about ninety when we hit the kitchen door. Dad looked up, shocked, like a comet had come through the window.

'Where the hell have you been?' he yelled.

Dorothy was there and so were the policemen.

'We were just going to have a cup of tea,' said the community copper.

'He's burnt it.'

'He's what?'

'Damian burnt the money.'

The policeman looked at me very hard and said, 'No harm done, then. That's what the government wanted to do in the first place. It's to do with the money supply.'

Dad went up to the front bedroom and opened the window. The voices in the Close poured in like water. He shouted, 'Listen!' And the voices stopped. 'The boys . . . one of the boys . . . has . . . down by the railway . . . he burnt the money. All of it.'

There was no sound in reply. It felt like there was no one out there. Then one voice – an old man's voice – went, 'When you say burnt, how badly?'

'What?'

'Only, if you can still see the serial numbers, apparently you can get remuneration at the bank.'

There was one more second of quiet and then suddenly a huge wave of voices exploded. There was shouting and yelling and pushing and shoving and the whole crowd of people poured out of the Close and through the gardens towards the railway line.

The police went after them due to concerns

about large numbers trespassing on railway property.

Which left Dad and me and Anthony and Dorothy. She was putting her coat on. She said, 'Well, it was fun while it lasted, eh?'

Dad said, 'Listen, if you want the car . . .'

'No, no. I love my little car. Thanks all the same.' She kissed him on the cheek, ruffled my hair and went to ruffle Anthony's but stopped herself just in time. And then she left.

We stood around saying nothing. I was waiting to hear her engine start up. But it didn't. Instead, the doorbell rang. It was her, back again. 'Look,' she said, 'there's no easy way to say this, but the fact is . . .' She put her hand inside her coat. 'I kept a bit back. For myself. It's yours really.'

And she put a wedge of money on the table.

Dad looked shocked at first, then pleased.

'It's six grand,' she said.

He went to the biscuit tin on the top shelf, levered it open and pulled out another wedge. He put it next to Dorothy's. She laughed. 'You crook!' she said.

'It's the dollars. It felt different somehow. Ten grand's worth.'

'Ten grand! That's worse than me! That's twice as bad as me, nearly!'

Anthony was emptying his dressing-gown pocket. He had a roll of notes the size of a Jaffa orange. 'I just liked having a wedge. The feel of it. It wasn't the money really. It was more like a stress ball.'

'How much?'

'Four thousand three hundred and forty-five.'

They stared at him. He shrugged. 'I enjoy counting it.'

Then they all three stared at me. I said, 'Well, don't look at me. I haven't got any.' They kept staring. 'I haven't!'

'Well, you could've put a bit by.'

'Well, I didn't.'

20

If our Anthony had been telling you this story, it would be the most unhappy ending ever. He would put, 'And so they failed to make proper use of their once-in-a-lifetime investment opportunity and they all regretted it ever after.'

Anthony regretted it hundreds of times every day. Every time we passed a shop window or saw an advert, he'd shake his head sadly, thinking of what might have been.

Because what actually happened was this. Since I was the only entirely honest member of the family, Dad said I could decide what we did with the money. And with 20,345 new euros we built 14 hand-dug wells in northern Nigeria.

Sometimes money can leave your hand and fall like water from a pipe on to the hot ground, and the dusty earth swallows it up and bursts into food and flowers for miles and miles around. And all the seeds and roots and lives that were lying dead in the ground spring all the way back to life.